Playing Outdoors in the Early Years

Also available from Continuum

Learning Through Play, Jacqueline Duncan and Madelaine Lockwood
Let's All Play – Activities for Communication, Language and Literacy, Jenny Roe
Physical Development in the Early Years, Lynda Woodfield
Reflective Playwork, Jacky Kilvington and Alison Wood
The Value of Play, Perry Else
Childminder's Guide to Play and Activities, Allison Lee

Playing Outdoors
in the Early Years

2nd edition

ROS GARRICK

continuum

Continuum International Publishing Group
The Tower Building   80 Maiden Lane
11 York Road   Suite 704
London SE1 7NX   New York NY 10038

www.continuumbooks.com

First published 2009
Reprinted 2011

British Library Cataloguing-in-Publication Data
A catalogue record for this book is available from the British Library.

ISBN: 978-1-8470-6547-6 (paperback)

Library of Congress Cataloging-in-Publication Data
Garrick, Ros.
Playing outdoors in the early years / Ros Garrick. – 2nd ed.
    p. cm.
Includes bibliographical references.
ISBN 978-1-84706-547-6 (pbk.)
1. Early childhood education–Activity programs. 2. Outdoor
recreation for children. I. Title.

LB1139.35.A37G37 2009
372.21--dc22

2009008263

Typeset by Kenneth Burnley, Wirral, Cheshire
Printed and bound in India

Contents

Acknowledgements		vii
Preface		viii
Introduction		ix

1 A rationale for outdoor play in early childhood education and care — **1**

Children's voices	1
Can you remember?	2
What are children's views?	4
Changing landscapes	6
Children's health	7
An environment for all kinds of learning	9
Gender issues	10

2 The place of the garden in the historical development of early childhood education — **13**

Friedrich Froebel	15
Margaret McMillan	16
Susan Isaacs	17
The historical tradition of play	18

3 Perspectives on young children and outdoor play — **21**

Psychological perspectives	22
Geographical perspectives	33
Sociological perspectives	35
Playwork perspectives	37

4 Outdoor play decisions 39

Programme structure 40
1- and 2-year-old quarrels: managing conflict 43
Unpredictable weather 46
All kinds of weather 49
Messy play 54
Gender 56
Inclusion 60
Listening to children 64
Health and safety 68

5 Planning an outdoor curriculum in the early years 73

Curriculum frameworks internationally 75
The observation and planning cycle 81
Long-term planning: designing the outdoor space 82
Defining spaces 84
Long-term planning: areas of provision 86
Evaluating long-term plans 96
Medium-term planning for outdoor learning 98
Short-term planning for outdoor learning 104
The adult role 106

6 Outdoor learning in early-years curricula internationally 115

The Villetta pre-school in Reggio Emilia 116
Forest Schools 117
Growing Schools in England 119

Sources of advice, guidance and support 121

References 123
Index 131

Acknowledgements

I would like to thank those I have worked with in schools, early-years settings and the advisory services in Leeds, Sheffield and Rotherham for sharing their practice and their thinking about outdoor play. In particular, I would like to thank the staff at Parklands Children's Centre in Leeds for their hospitality and generosity in allowing me to learn from their practice. The photographs in this book are of the very well used outdoor areas at Parklands, both the area for 2- to 3-year-olds and the area for 3- to 5-year-olds. I would also like to thank colleagues at Sheffield Hallam University for their encouragement and constructive comments. Finally, I would like to thank my family for their support and good humour.

Preface

This book is for all those training to work with young children in early childhood education and care settings. It presents a rationale for outdoor play as an essential feature of the early childhood curriculum and explores how effective practice flows from an understanding of research and theoretical perspectives. These include perspectives on children's development; perspectives on children's agency in their social worlds; perspectives on the role of adults in children's learning; and perspectives on the development of environments for play. The outdoor curriculum raises several challenging issues for practitioners which are recognized and explored. However, the book also includes many examples of practice that exemplify the power of high-quality outdoor play and outdoor experiences to enhance the lives of children, their families and their communities.

Introduction

You can play in the secret house out there! Do you know how? Get some of those cardboard pieces you see around sometimes, you know? Cover the ends of the tunnel with them and then play and do anything you want, even hide and seek! There are monsters and ghosts in the tunnel! (But just for fun.) (Diana Municipal Pre-school 1990, p. 2)

The pioneers of early childhood education, including Froebel, Montessori and Margaret McMillan, placed a special emphasis on the provision of outdoor play and learning environments for young children (Bilton 2002). Many contemporary practitioners, working in different cultures and traditions, also strive to promote high-quality outdoor learning opportunities for young children. At the Diana pre-school, in the Italian town of Reggio Emilia, for example, 5- and 6-year-olds take pleasure in describing the fun of physical, imaginative and creative play in their school grounds to incoming 3-year-olds (Diana Municipal Pre-school 1990). In Wales, children from a reception class and special teaching facility in an area of social and economic disadvantage experience the wildness of the natural world as they explore a challenging woodland environment (Maynard 2007). As a further example, babies who are crawling and learning to walk in the garden of the Universal Studios Child Development Center in Los Angeles, California, enjoy rich sensory experiences, including the textures and changing temperatures of smooth boulders (Curtis and Carter 2003). Each example is evidence of children engaged in rich, holistic learning experiences in an outdoor environment.

There are many further examples of early-years practitioners developing challenging experiential education for young children in outdoor settings. However, such practice is far from universal. Even where statutory guidance identifies outdoor play as an essential feature of the early childhood curriculum (DCSF 2008; Welsh

Assembly Government 2008), differences in levels of provision may be significant. In England, for example, a recent review of childcare and early education provision identified much successful provision, including provision for babies and toddlers, where 'outdoor areas are made accessible to all children and are used in all types of weather' (Ofsted 2008, p. 24). However, currently there is no requirement in England to develop outdoor areas as a condition of registration, only an expectation that providers without outdoor space will use communal facilities such as parks, and these can be some distance from settings. In a study (Mooney et al. 2008) of approaches to health in early-years settings in England, some interviewees described the challenge of promoting physical activity where settings had limited or no outdoor play space. Even in settings where outdoor areas exist, children's use may be infrequent, the quality of environments poor, and/or opportunities for learning limited. In a recent Canadian study (Herrington 2008), researchers asked 78 early childhood educators from 14 settings to evaluate their outdoor play space, and 79 per cent identified a lack of sensori stimuli such as plants or water. In addition, many participants identified an excess of concrete and asphalt, which tended to create a 'cold, hard place that was very loud and often lacking in colour' (Herrington 2008, p. 75). Such limitations suggest that the potential of outdoor play and learning in accessible and high-quality play spaces is not universally recognized.

Commitment to outdoor play in the early years can vary at both policy and practice levels. Countries vary in their policy commitment to outdoor play in ways that are likely to relate to longstanding curricular traditions. For example, the Organization for Economic Co-operation and Development (OECD) thematic review of policy in this area (OECD 2006) identifies an early education tradition, in France and several English-speaking countries, which focused on 'readiness for school'. In these countries, national policy is more likely to identify indoors as the main learning environment, designating outdoors as primarily a recreational space. In contrast, countries such as Norway, Denmark and Sweden, influenced by the Nordic social pedagogy tradition, are more likely to accord 'equal pedagogical importance' (OECD 2006, p. 141) to both kinds of space, with a consequent financial commitment to the outdoors.

Cultural traditions influence individual practitioners and managers, alongside policy recommendations and prescription. Maynard and Waters (2007, p. 262), reporting on the reluctance of a group of Welsh early-years teachers to provide outdoor play in wet and wintry weather, hypothesize the influence of a Welsh and British cultural identity that can include 'cultural resistance to the perceived discomforts of the outdoor environment and a concern to protect children, and themselves, from these discomforts'. Ouvry (2000) examines reasons commonly given for limited outdoor play provision in some English settings, highlighting weather conditions as well as safety and staffing ratios, health issues and the difficulties of access to outdoor space. Association of Teachers and Lecturers (ATL) research findings (Ellis 2002; Adams et al. 2004) identify further issues, suggesting cultural traditions as a barrier to legislated change. Researchers questioned ATL members in England and Wales about the implementation of new statutory guidance with a high focus on outdoor learning. Despite the official privileging of outdoor learning, 61 per cent of teachers identified the use of outdoor areas as problematic, and a significant number reported a lack of management support for outdoor play and inadequate guidance for the development of outdoor learning environments. Different cultural traditions and recurring contradictions between policy and practice suggest that outdoor play remains a contested feature of early-years education and care.

This book begins by examining the rationale for outdoor play in early childhood education and care (Chapter 1). The main focus is on children up to 5 years but with some consideration of outdoor play in education and care settings for children up to 7 years. The book moves on to consider the special place of the garden and outdoor experiences in the historical development of the sector (Chapter 2). Following this, the book examines key theories that support an understanding of young children, and considers the implications for learning and teaching outdoors (Chapter 3). Chapter 4 examines some of the issues related to young children's experiences and learning in outdoor environments. In subsequent chapters, approaches to planning for children's development and learning are discussed, and examples of outdoor learning in early childhood curricula internationally are introduced. The book concludes with information about organizations and agencies that can support the development of practice in this challenging area.

1 | A rationale for outdoor play in early childhood education and care

We need to be full of wonder at what children say and do, and hence curious to continue listening to and hearing what they say and do. (Dahlberg et al. 2006, p. 135)

Children's voices

As policy-makers, researchers and practitioners work through the implications of recent international and national laws and conventions relating to children's rights, many are striving to listen more attentively to children's voices. Internationally, the UN Convention on the Rights of the Child 1989, in particular Articles 12 and 13, establishes an expectation that adults working with and for children should take account of children's distinctive perspectives, including those of the very young (Franklin 2002). Additionally, aspects of national legislation reinforce this approach. For example, the Childcare Act 2006 for England and Wales includes a new duty for local authorities (LAs) to take account of the views of young children and their parents when developing and evaluating childcare services. Thomas (2001) identifies three compelling arguments that underpin the recent emphasis on children's rights: when we, as adults, listen to children's voices, we are respecting the child's right to be heard; we enhance children's lives; and we can improve the quality of policies and practice.

For students and practitioners examining the rationale for outdoor play in the early-years curriculum, this is a helpful approach. We need to attend to children's voices, as well as curriculum documents and official guidance. However, as adults we all too easily lose touch with the world as seen through children's eyes, even when working in close proximity to children. As we seek children's perspectives on outdoor play, personal memories can provide a powerful starting point.

Can you remember?

REFLECTION POINT

What were your favourite places as a young child?

Choose one special place:

- What sensory experiences can you remember? What sounds, smells, tastes, textures, colours, movement?

- What emotions can you remember?

- What people can you remember?

- What activities can you remember?

A group of undergraduate students on an Early Childhood Studies course was invited to reflect on five places they particularly liked and five they particularly disliked as children. Students and their tutor shared many happy and exciting memories. They also shared memories that evoked past feelings of anxiety, fear, and, in many cases, unpleasant boredom.

It is salutary to note some of the disliked places and experiences common to even happy childhoods. Many students recalled dreary, interminable shopping expeditions, with endless queues in shops, banks and at bus-stops. Some recalled constraining visits to relatives, cooped up indoors with little to do. This reminds us that much of young children's lives is spent in adult worlds, tuned in to adult needs and desires that may not match their own. Less tangible but no less intense were the memories of fear and anxiety attached to dark and sometimes hidden places: under beds, on the landing or down a cellar. This reminds us that early childhood is a period of intense emotions of both a positive and negative kind.

Among the shared lists of favourite places, outdoor play spaces featured strongly. Many students recalled pleasurable experiences in parks and gardens. Mature students and their tutor shared additional memories of play beyond these domesticated confines. Memories dating back to the 1950s and 1960s were of wilder, more private places, for example fields, woods and streams, sometimes miles beyond the controlling gaze of adults. These recollections of wild places were rare among the younger students and this provides anecdotal support for the view that outdoor play experiences have become increasingly constrained for children in the economically rich, industrialized countries of the North (Morrow 2002). There were clear differences across the generations, but nearly everyone remembered at least one private and secret place that evoked powerful feelings of pleasure. Special places included a wild patch under fruit trees at the end of a long garden, a tiny space behind a garden shed and a spacious den hidden within tangled, overgrown bushes.

In a reflective account on memory and outdoor learning, Waite (2007) considers how positive emotions of this kind, linked to reconstructed, early memories of outdoor play, may act as a significant motivator of lifelong learning. In a study that included a survey of practitioners working with either pre-school (2–5 years) or primary schoolchildren, 241 respondents (72 per cent of the sample) shared memories of outdoor play as children. The majority (195) shared mainly positive feelings, as with earlier studies, and only six reported negative experiences. Most positive memories of the outdoors included a social aspect, often with family members, including both siblings and adults. In terms of context, adults most often reported pleasurable memories of natural contexts, particularly woodlands and trees, but also farms and gardens. Linked to these natural contexts, active investigation featured as a positive feature of many memories, with 36 adults remembering activities with animals of varying sizes, 'from worms to horses' (Waite 2007, p. 339). Challenging and adventurous activities, for example exploring places, climbing trees and lighting fires, also featured among adults' positive memories. These findings suggest some of the characteristics of early, outdoor experiences that are remembered vividly and often with positive effect.

As a final example, the salience of natural outdoor places and things for adults is encapsulated in the striking art work (Illustration 1.1) created by staff and parents at Parklands Children's Centre in Leeds. Following a visit to Leeds City Art Gallery, a member of staff worked with parents to create the wheel, with each contributor selecting a natural object or objects of significance for their lives. These objects were either related to memories of childhood or relevant to current lives.

When planning outdoor experiences for young children, it is

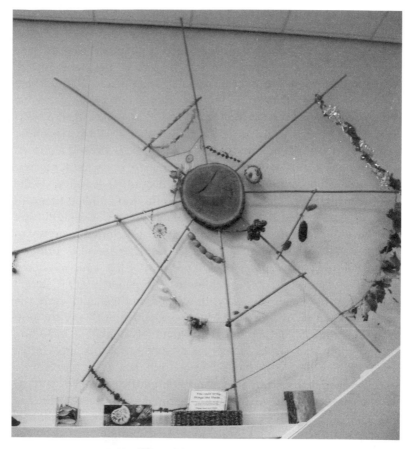

Illustration 1.1: Art work

important to reflect on remembered outdoor experiences and the special feelings retained by adults for natural places and things.

What are children's views?

Informal research and more formal studies (Waite 2007) highlight outdoor play in childhood as representing some of our most salient and pleasurable memories as adults. Perhaps the adult's rose-tinted glasses reshape memories and play a part in creating such pleasurable images. However, studies of children in the here-and-now provide support for this view, offering detailed accounts of the outdoor places and experiences that young children like, as well as

---

REFLECTION POINT

What are children's favourite outdoor places?

Think of a baby, toddler or young child who you know well.

- What sensory experiences do they enjoy outdoors, for example sounds, smells, tastes, textures, colours, movement?

- What actions or activities do they choose to repeat outdoors?

- What emotions do they show outdoors?

- Who do they choose to play with outdoors?

---

the places they dislike. While relatively few studies focus primarily on the views of children under 7, wider studies often include this age group.

Hart's (1979) important early study of children's outdoor play in a small American town was framed within geographical perspectives on childhood. Hart was interested in the ways in which children used the immediate and wider outdoor environment of the town in which to play and socialize. As an ethnographic researcher, he lived as a member of the close community for two years, studying both the children's use of space and their personal feelings about place. Hart used a combination of traditional and innovative methods, including methods that engaged children as co-researchers. An important finding was the importance that children attached to making special places of their own, the 'forts and houses' they regularly constructed in hidden places.

More recently, Millward and Whey (1997) studied children's play on English housing estates, seeking data to inform urban planning. Observations and interviews highlight children's enjoyment of both physically active play and quieter games. In particular, children value the opportunities to socialize and make choices afforded by diverse environments. This valuing of social experience outdoors echoes the emphasis on pleasurable social experience encapsulated in adult memories of outdoor play (Waite 2007).

Turning to young children's perspectives on play in early-years settings, Clark and Moss (2001, 2005) have developed a methodolog-ically innovative approach (the Mosaic approach) that brings together a mosaic of research methods and invites children's partici-pation. Methods include observations, interviews, tours of a setting, map-making, and children's photographs used in various ways, for example to elicit children's reflections on their nursery. Findings from a number of studies using this approach (Clark 2007) highlight the special and positive feelings that young children sometimes have for what adults perceive to be very ordinary places. For Gary, aged 3, a circular bench on a small piece of grass had the special properties of a magical cave, while a small piece of ground by the side of the shed was another important place (Clark and Moss 2001). Identify-ing patterns across studies, Clark (2007, pp. 356–8) highlights the value that children give to 'private places', to enjoy alone or with a small group of friends, from which they can survey the world. Children also value 'social spaces' providing a venue for child-led activities, 'personal spaces' with links to the child's own identity, and 'imaginary spaces' which can be the focus for imaginative games and stories. A single outdoor space may be rich in potential for different kinds of experience and feelings. These studies present strong voices from children, evidencing the importance of outdoor places and experiences in their lives.

They also highlight the importance of finding ways to enable children to communicate their own perspectives on outdoor play. Children's views can inform our efforts to improve the effectiveness of outdoor provision. A number of other interlinking factors support arguments for an outdoor play curriculum. These will be discussed in the rest of this chapter.

Changing landscapes

Karen Miller (1989, p. 9) describes the sensual pleasures of outdoor play during a childhood lived on the edge of a Michigan lake, 'digging, sorting stones, finding snails, making mountains, rivers and dams, drawing pictures with a stick, dribbling mud and enjoy-ing all the different textures at my fingertips'. She comments regret-fully that contemporary children have diminished opportunities for such independent exploration of natural landscapes.

Anecdotal observations such as this gain support from environ-mental sociologists who study children's attitudes to the natural

world. Nabhan (1994b) reports that even children living in close proximity to nature have diminished first-hand experience of the natural
world. Many Anglo, Hispanic and American Indian children, living
in American country and desert areas, are keenly interested in conservation issues. However, they gain more information about
plants, animals and landscapes from the media and school than from
exploring local environments. These children are far less likely to
explore natural spaces than previous generations. Nabhan (1994b,
p. 11) presents the experience of children in the city as bleaker still:

> . . . an increasingly large proportion of inner-city children will
> never gain adequate access to unpeopled places, neither food-
> producing field nor wild lands. They will grow up in a world
> where asphalt, concrete and plaster cover more ground than
> shade-providing shrubs and their resident songbirds.

Davis and Elliot (2004) argue that the disappearance of opportunities for engagement with the natural world may have significant
implications for children's environmental understanding. They
advocate this as an important concern for early childhood educators
who have a responsibility to ensure that young children gain direct
experience of the natural world to nurture a sense of environmental
responsibility.

Nevertheless, we should be wary of idealizing the childhood landscapes of the past. The history of early childhood education includes
many educators who were committed to providing the experience
of natural environments for children growing up in bleak and unhealthy cities (Bilton 2002). Given commitment and imagination,
practitioners today can similarly develop outdoor environments that
nourish children's environmental understanding. This is an important part of the rationale for outdoor play.

Children's health

The impact of changing landscapes on lifestyles is one of a number
of factors contributing to concerns for children's health and well-
being in the twenty-first century. Gill (2008) explains how environmental and social change in the United Kingdom, including increase
in car ownership, decreasing local, green spaces and the fragmenta-
tion of communities, has limited opportunities for children from

across social classes to participate in outdoor play and activities. A *British Medical Journal* (*BMJ*) (2001) editorial argues that such environmental change, alongside changes to family eating patterns and an increase in television viewing among young children, has contributed to an epidemic of childhood obesity and related health problems across England, the United States and other countries. In the United States, a form of diabetes that usually appears in adulthood is appearing for the first time among overweight children. Shell's (2003) review of research also demonstrates the link between lifestyle and health, with clear associations between the hours of television watched and children's risk of becoming overweight or obese. Childhood asthma is another serious and growing health problem, again a negative consequence of changes in environments and technology (Robb 2001).

Much evidence suggests that lifestyle attitudes, in particular diet and patterns of activity, are shaped in childhood. Mooney et al. (2008) explain how early-years settings may have an important role to play, alongside national campaigns, in reversing current British trends. However, these authors do highlight a need for additional resources if early-years settings are to play a significant role in the achievement of 'Be Healthy' outcomes, as one of the set of five outcomes for children and young people that make up the *Every Child Matters: Change for Children* (DfES 2004) programme. Similarly, in responding to the obesity epidemic in the United States, Burdette and Whitaker (2005) argue for the need for health professionals to share with parents the importance of unstructured, physically active outdoor play in early childhood, arguing that 'play' is a more motivating and positive term for use with parents than 'exercise' or 'sport'. These terms may carry negative connotations of failed weight reduction efforts for adults. Burdette and Whitaker (2005) also argue for a new emphasis on physically active play in early-years settings, for both physical health and improved cognitive, social and emotional well-being. Well-planned outdoor spaces can significantly increase the opportunities for young children to engage in physically active play.

Children with health problems and/or limited experience of active play can lack confidence in their own physical skills and appear unmotivated to engage in active play. For these children, encouragement to participate in sociable, group activities, for example a 'Bear Hunt' obstacle course (Drake 2001) or large-scale construction play, can build confidence, self-esteem and positive dispositions towards active play. In addition, snacks, such as pieces of raw or dried fruit, raw vegetables, breadsticks or cheese, eaten picnic style in the outside area, can reinforce messages about healthy lifestyles. A concern to take positive action in the face of societal pressures undermining our children's health, is an important part of the rationale for outdoor play.

An environment for all kinds of learning

Outdoor environments afford rich opportunities for physical development and learning. They provide opportunities for other valuable experiences less easily or effectively provided indoors. Baldock (2001), for example, suggests that the child's early experience of exploring large outdoor spaces may be critical to the development of spatial abilities. English guidance (DCSF 2008) corresponds to this by recommending that children are encouraged to use everyday words to describe position when playing on outdoor apparatus or following pathways, and a study by Williams (1994) provides support for this guidance. Examining young children's talk about play on a nursery climbing frame, this study provides evidence of one child making marked progress in the use of language to explore concepts of speed, size and length over a six-month period of outdoor play.

Baldock (2001) also argues that outdoor spaces provide children with greater opportunities for independence than more adult-controlled indoor spaces. Stephenson's (2002) research in a childcare setting in New Zealand supports this view of the outdoors as a less adult-controlled environment than the indoors. For example, children outdoors were seen to be less subject to adult-led routines than indoors. Additionally, younger children outdoors had more control over the movement of natural materials such as sand, water and bark chips, play which practitioners viewed as supporting transporting schema, and older children had more freedom to move large-scale equipment such as construction materials. Nind's (2001) action research, focused on language development in an early-years unit, identifies another positive aspect of independent play outdoors. She suggests that children may be more confident in their use of language outdoors than indoors because of a perceived independence from adult control.

Edgington (2002) presents a further argument for the distinctive

---

REFLECTION POINT

Think of a small-scale experience or activity suitable for a baby, toddler or young child indoors:

- a sensory experience;

- an exploratory activity;

- a creative activity.

How could the experience or activity be transformed by moving it outdoors and planning for a significant increase in scale?

---

quality of outdoor environments, suggesting that the outdoors allows for a valuable change of scale in children's play.

Children's exploration of percussion instruments exemplifies the potential of an increase in scale. Constraints on volume and space disappear outdoors, so that children can enjoy a wider range of instruments and explore the sounds of large-scale percussion instruments designed for the outdoors. These and other distinctive qualities of outdoor environments, discussed throughout this book, support the case for outdoor play.

Gender issues

Gender issues provide a final element of the rationale. The education of boys is a fiercely debated issue in many countries, including the UK. At the end of secondary schooling, girls are outperforming boys, and concern for boys' academic achievements is growing, although its significance is contested when set in the context of differences relating to social disadvantage (Connolly 2004). The British government has identified an urgent need to 'challenge the laddish anti-learning culture' of secondary education (Henry 2003, p. 16). However, concern for the achievements of secondary school students may come too late for effective action. In England, where an early start to school is the norm (Sharp 2003) some gender-related differences in achievement are evident in children as young as 4 and 5 years (Connolly 2004).

It is useful to consider the evidence for early behavioural differences that may relate to approaches to learning and subsequent achievement. Despite some change in attitudes over recent decades, boys are often stereotyped as more aggressive, dominant, confident and active than girls. Smith et al. (2003), reporting a study of child rearing across six cultures (Kenya, Japan, India, the Philippines, Mexico and the USA), report findings that match some of the stereotypes, with boys on average demonstrating more aggressive and dominant behaviour than girls, as well as higher levels of rough-and-tumble play. It is important to note that these differences in behaviour often related to different socialization pressures on children. For example, girls were often required to do more nurturing tasks than boys, such as caring for younger siblings. Additionally, although studies may report differences across groups, there are also likely to be significant variations in behaviour within any group of girls or boys.

However, given some evidence of early gender-related behavioural differences (Smith et al. 2003), over-formalized approaches in early education, including a lack of opportunities for physically active play, may be problematic for some children, particularly boys. Meade (2006) describes the importance of outdoor spaces in New Zealand settings and the links to an early childhood curriculum aim to develop positive dispositions towards learning for infants, toddlers and pre-school children. The New Zealand curriculum focus is on learning dispositions rather than pre-specified learning outcomes, and Meade suggests that children's engagement is particularly evident in outdoor spaces. An outdoor curriculum, offering opportunities for active play, exploration and the development of the language skills that underpin later academic development, may have an important part to play in supporting learning dispositions for both boys and girls. This provides a final and significant strand in the rationale for outdoor play.

Further Reading

Edgington, M. (2002), *The Great Outdoors*. London: Early Education.

Waite, S. (2007), '"Memories are made of this": some reflections on outdoor learning and recall', in *Education 3–13*. 35 (4), pp. 333–47.

2 | The place of the garden in the historical development of early childhood education

How often in later life will their thoughts go back to the first garden, which surely must be as rich as we can make it. (McMillan, in Bradford Education, 1995, p. 8)

There is a strong, contemporary case for the value of the outdoor curriculum in early childhood settings. Before looking at the details of implementation, it is helpful to examine two distinct strands within the historical development of outdoor play. The first strand is represented by the playground or yard of the elementary school tradition that can be traced back to the nineteenth century (Thomson 2005); the second is the garden of the nursery school tradition. The introductory discussion focuses on the United Kingdom.

From the end of the nineteenth century into the early years of the twentieth century, many 3–5-year-olds attended elementary schools. Board of Education records for 1900 show 43 per cent of this age group in schools that offered poor, working-class women a cheap form of childminding (Bilton 2002). Although children joined designated 'baby' classes, the system made no concession to their age or stage of development; group exercises in bleak schoolyards provided only limited relief from regimented learning in cramped and stuffy classrooms (Steedman 1990).

The ideology of this tradition continued to exert an influence on British infant and primary education into the twentieth century. It shaped a utilitarian view of the curriculum, a view that emphasized the basic skills of literacy and numeracy, and a didactic approach to teaching (Anning 1997). Many infant and primary schools, steeped in this tradition, maintain a similarly utilitarian view of outdoor play. Outdoor 'playtimes' are times for children to 'let off steam' between periods of 'work' of a mainly sedentary nature. Despite curriculum guidance relating to the youngest children in English schools (DCSF 2008), this remains a typical pattern for 5–7-year-olds, as well as for some 4-year-olds. A seminal study by Titman (1994) highlighted how many children play on featureless playgrounds or fields, with few play resources. More recently, Thomson's (2005) research into children's use of playgrounds identified high levels of adult prescription on children's use of space, limiting opportunities for social and physical play. In addition, within this tradition, staffing levels provide for only basic levels of adult supervision, with limited opportunities for adult–child interaction.

REFLECTION POINT

Think of a school or nursery playground that appears to match playgrounds of the elementary school tradition. What opportunities are there for:

- sensory experience;

- exploratory experience;

- creative experience

- movement experience;

- social experience?

How effectively does this environment support young children's learning and development?

How well does it promote young children's well-being?

In contrast, from the early nineteenth century onwards, a tradition of nursery education shaped a very different approach to outdoor play across the US and Europe (Bilton 2002). There are significant differences in the ideologies and practice of key figures within this nursery tradition, as discussed below. However, there is an important continuity in the emphasis placed on the garden and its identification as a special place for young children's play and learning.

Friedrich Froebel

Friedrich Froebel's educational practice and theories, developed during the first half of the nineteenth century, were influential in shaping the early history of the nursery garden. Growing up in Germany, and with a boyhood interest in nature, Froebel began work as an apprentice in forestry and later studied biology. His knowledge and intense love of nature, as well as a deeply spiritual approach to experience, informed an innovative approach to teaching. This was crystallized in his work with very young children in the later years of his life (Dudek 2000).

The garden was at the centre of Froebel's educational work and, in his first kindergarten, it was a very real experience in children's lives. However, the term 'kindergarten' also served as a metaphor for the nurture of the young and, for Froebel, symbolized an ideal social order. To encourage children to grow up in harmony with nature, Froebel gave each child his or her own small garden to tend. Individual and communal gardens provided flowers and vegetables, which were often given to neighbours. Children were encouraged to observe plants and wildlife in the garden and were taken on excursions into the surrounding countryside. The key aim was to nurture children's spiritual awareness. Froebel's garden was also a place for exercise and play. He devised special songs and movement games for outdoor play, the forerunners of contemporary action rhymes and circle games (Herrington 2001).

Froebel's radical educational theories inspired many followers, initially in Germany but, in the following decades, across Europe, Japan and North America. Until the late nineteenth century, an expanding kindergarten movement remained faithful to Froebel's romantic ideals. However, the history of gardens within this tradition is a complex one and, in the United States, Froebel's spiritual ideals and practice were changed significantly as kindergartens became integrated into the public school system (Herrington 2001).

In recent decades, some American architects have sought inspiration in Froebel's ideas and there has been a revived interest in the therapeutic value of gardens for children (Herrington 2001). Given children's diminishing levels of experience of nature and the high incidence of mental health problems in some communities (Mooney et al. 2008), Froebel's focus on the garden as key to young children's spiritual development has continuing contemporary relevance.

Margaret McMillan

Margaret McMillan worked in England during the last decades of the nineteenth and the first decades of the twentieth centuries and was influenced by Froebelian thinking. She had a diverse career in which children, in particular working-class children, provided a central focus for her work. Growing up in the US and Scotland, she was a prolific journalist, fiction writer, adult educator, socialist politician and social reformer. Her most significant achievements were founding a school medical service within an emergent welfare state and developing a nursery school in the slums of south London (Steedman 1990).

From 1884, working as an Independent Labour Party representative on a Bradford school board, Margaret McMillan gained extensive experience of the harsh, unhealthy home and working lives of working-class children. She also gained experience of the bleak elementary school tradition that did little to ameliorate these lives. Following a move to London in the early 1900s, she pioneered a new children's clinic in Deptford, and here came to understand the healing effects of outdoor environments and their potential for transforming young working-class lives. After running successful camp schools for older children, Margaret McMillan's interest turned to children under 5 years old. The Deptford nursery school grew out of the first open-air baby camp, and it was here Margaret McMillan developed her thinking about the nursery garden (Steedman 1990).

Over the next two decades, an extensive and beautiful garden was created for the children of this impoverished south London community. The key elements were shelter provided by varied trees, bushes and terraced rock gardens; the sensory experiences of a herb garden; a vegetable garden providing food for the children's meals; cultivated and wildflower gardens; climbing equipment and sandpits; and a heap, for children to explore assorted natural and manufactured objects. The garden was designed to be on view to the community, to provide pleasure and an educational experience for parents as well as children (Bradford Education 1995).

As a highly educated woman, Margaret McMillan was conversant with the most recent ideas about physical maturation, language development and stages in children's psychological development. The nursery garden was designed as an arena within which scientific and political ideas about childhood, in particular working-class childhood, might be explored (Steedman 1990).

Margaret McMillan's work focused on children's physical and emotional well-being as prerequisites for intellectual development. This focus, as well as the contribution of the nursery garden to the lives of a community, has continuing relevance. The third *State of London's Children Report* (McNeish and Scott 2007) identifies significant numbers of children living in poverty today and confirms the continuing negative impact of poverty on child health and well-being, including children's mental health. It remains important for practitioners to value outdoor environments for the part they play in promoting children's health and emotional well-being, as well as improving the quality of life for families and communities.

Susan Isaacs

Susan Isaacs is a third important figure in this tradition. Working in a very different social context, with highly advantaged children, Susan Isaacs opened the Malting House School in a large house in Cambridge in 1924. She was a trained infant teacher, as well as a qualified philosopher, psychologist and practising psychoanalyst. These distinctive perspectives contributed to the observations and analyses of children's learning that informed her teaching at the small, private school. By the end of three years at the school, Susan Isaacs had an extensive set of observations of children's play, investigations and thinking that were to provide the basis for three influential books about young children's learning (Drummond 2000).

The children, mostly aged between 2 and 8 years, had an unusual degree of freedom at the school, with opportunities to explore expansive outdoor environments. The garden and outdoor buildings represented the main part of the learning environment, and some of Susan Isaac's most interesting and unusual writing focuses on children's experiences outdoors. The outdoor environment was richly resourced and included areas that stimulated different kinds of thinking: spaces for bonfires, bricks in a building area, and an unusual seesaw that had movable weights fastened underneath. At different times it included a number of common, domestic pets and some more unusual ones, for example snakes, silkworms and salamanders. Alongside the animals, there were plants and fruit trees, providing a diverse natural environment (Drummond 2000).

Susan Isaacs' writings evidence the ways in which children's intense investigations and thinking about biological and spiritual concepts, including death, can be supported by unconstrained experiences outdoors. Her writings, for example the account of children burying and digging up a dead pet rabbit, are likely to shock contemporary readers (Drummond 2000). Susan Isaacs moved from her teaching role to a career at the Institute of Education, London, where she had a significant influence on child-centred, early education (Graham 2008). Her writings about the educational experiment at the Malting House School have continuing relevance and can support our understandings of the ways in which vivid first-hand experience outdoors nourishes early cognitive and affective development.

The historical tradition of play

Discussion has focused on these three of many important figures in the history of early childhood education because their work represents three important strands in the history of outdoor play and the nursery garden, with continuing relevance. Froebel represents an insistence on the spiritual needs of the young child; Margaret Mc-Millan represents an emphasis on children's physical health and emotional well-being; and Susan Isaacs represents a preoccupation with the young child's intense intellectual and emotional life.

REFLECTION POINT

Think back to your childhood experiences outdoors.

Can you remember special outdoor places and experiences that contributed to your

- spiritual needs;
- physical health;
- emotional well-being;
- intellectual life;
- emotional life?

Bruce (2005) and others have invoked shared principles from the historical tradition of play as an inspiration for contemporary early-years practitioners. However, Wood and Attfield (2005) warn against invoking this tradition uncritically in support of a play-based curriculum. They argue that, first, the tradition includes a mix of disparate and often contradictory ideas; second, the pioneers of nursery education developed their thinking in very different social and cultural contexts from those of today; and third, the tradition cannot substitute for theoretical accounts of play and young children's learning.

There are, however, continuities as well as discontinuities in childhood experience; and the preoccupations of these three figures – Froebel, McMillan and Isaacs – have some continuing relevance. The next chapter examines theoretical accounts of play and young children's learning, to support a deeper understanding of the role of play and, in particular, outdoor play and experience in young children's lives.

Further Reading

Bilton, H. (2002), *Outdoor Play in the Early Years: Management and Innovation* (2nd edn). London: David Fulton.

Dudek, M. (2000), *Kindergarten Architecture: Space for the Imagination* (2nd edn). London: Spon Press.

3 | Perspectives on young children and outdoor play

Outdoor play settings may be the one place where children can independently orchestrate their own negotiations with the physical and social environment and gain the clarity of selfhood necessary to navigate later in life. (Perry 2001, p. 118)

Introducing discussion of the concept of play, Sutton-Smith (1997, p. 1) makes the point that, although play is something we have all experienced and know something about, we find it very hard to provide clear or reliable definitions of play and to agree exactly what play is: 'There is little agreement among us, and much ambiguity.' He goes on to examine the many different forms of animal, child and adult play that take place in a wide range of settings, including sports stadiums, theatres, carnival processions, casinos, and children's playgrounds. This book is about young children's play and primarily about play in outdoor spaces in early-years settings. The extract introducing this section provides one perspective on young children's play, a sociological perspective that draws on understandings of young children's peer cultures. However, when focusing on young children's play, there are many different ways of understanding play. The perspectives of developmental psychology, established over the first decades of the twentieth century, have often governed thinking about young children and early education (Walsh 2005; Frost et al. 2008). However, Raban et al. (2003) suggest that, to acknowledge the complexity of children's development and learning, we need to consider the contribution made by multiple theoretical perspectives.

Raban et al. (2003) identify five psychological perspectives on children's learning that support practitioners in developing a range of 'practice styles'. In addition, there are other important perspectives that can deepen and sometimes challenge our understanding of children's lives, including their play in education and care settings.

The intersecting and rich perspectives of sociology and geography are important, as are recent playwork perspectives on children and early childhood education. Frost et al. (2008, p. 57) explain why it is important for practitioners to draw on a range of theories to understand children's play and learning, and to make appropriate decisions about practice: 'We must know the various theories that provide us with ways of choosing what to look for and with ways of making sense of what we see. Theories of play become our lenses for observation and reflection.' The following section considers a range of perspectives on children's play in outdoor environments and examines critically the implications for practice.

Psychological perspectives

The growing and maturing child

Beginning with the philosophical writing of Jean-Jacques Rousseau (1712–78), the garden has provided a recurring metaphor for the nurturing of young children's natural growth within educational settings. Biological models similarly place emphasis on what they conceptualize as the early and natural unfolding of development (Raban et al. 2003). Arnold Gesell and Myrtle McGraw carried out extensive naturalistic observations of children in the 1920s and 1930s and were the first to chart the stages of children's physical development, from early movement patterns to mature patterns of behaviour. Gesell extended this approach to cognitive and social development, again theorizing that children passed through a sequence of biologically determined stages. Gesell's primary emphasis on the biological programming of development is not widely accepted today. However, Gesell's work was important in establishing normative guidelines for key aspects of development including play, supporting parents of the time in anticipating their children's milestones. Reviewing the history of child development research, Parke (2004) acknowledges Gesell as a pioneer in terms of both methodology and theory.

Gesell was committed to providing advice to parents, and today a maturational perspective is often the commonsense approach of parents and educators, reflected in our language by such common sayings as, 'She's just going through a phase.' In terms of implications for practice, the maturational perspective suggests a mainly monitoring role for the adult during outdoor play, with development left to proceed at its own pace (Raban et al. 2003).

Monitoring remains a common approach to young children's physical development outdoors in some settings. However, Woodward and Yun (2001) argue that non-interventionist approaches may limit children's optimal development. In a study focused on the gross motor skills of young children in an American Headstart programme, they found that just over half the children had age-appropriate skills, while a significant minority had less developed skills. The free-play programme offered outdoor play but little or no adult interaction around physical skills, and it appeared to be ineffective in promoting the physical development of this group

A maturational perspective on physical development may be satisfactory for some children, where 3–5-year-olds have opportunities for physically active play and children are motivated to engage in active play. However, for many children this approach is inadequate. It underestimates the adult role with the youngest children in creating comfortable spaces and in encouraging new physical actions outdoors, in particular rolling, sitting up, crawling and pulling up. For older children, a maturational approach underplays the adult role in nurturing children's dispositions to engage in physically active play outdoors through imaginative, varied and differentiated programmes of play and activities (Gallahue and Ozmun 1998).

The pre-school child

Educators working within a readiness perspective emphasize the early years as a period of preparation for formal schooling and they construct the young child as a 'pre-school' child. Readiness perspectives grew out of biological models of development but placed a new emphasis on the role of experience in development. Informed by the behaviourist theories of the 1950s, the readiness perspective ascribes a more active role to the adult. This approach suggests that adults should, first, identify deficits in children's experience that prevent readiness for formal learning, and second, introduce activities to hasten readiness (Raban et al. 2003).

Direct instruction, implemented with sensitivity to children's interests and intentions, has an important part to play in early childhood settings (Siraj-Blatchford et al. 2002). McNaughton and

Williams (2009) suggest that 'telling and instructing' can play a part in teaching children safety and social rules, and in promoting new knowledge and skills. Outdoors, practitioners can use 'telling and instructing' very purposefully as a commentary to engage babies in ongoing events. For example, drawing a baby's attention to an outdoor mobile, a practitioner might say, 'I'm tapping the mobile. Listen to the jingles. Again?' With toddlers and pre-school children, a 'telling and instructing' approach is essential for some health and safety purposes. For example, when refilling a bird feeder, a practitioner with toddlers might need to explain clearly that the food is not for children to eat. There is also a place for a 'telling and instructing' approach with older children, for example to teach new games such as a new circle game, or new skills such as putting on a jacket.

There are many relevant uses for this approach outdoors as one of a range of strategies. However, the readiness perspective, as a dominant approach, has been mainly associated with the elementary school tradition in terms of outdoor play. Here, adults provide 'letting off steam' breaks between longer periods of formal learning or provide short play periods as rewards for appropriate behaviour and learning. This model is exemplified by the Miami pre-schools that were the focus of the Oxford Preschool Research Project (Sylva et al. 1980). Children in these centres engaged in short but intense periods of physical activity outdoors between longer periods of 'school readiness' activities. However, the children demonstrated little of the intellectually challenging behaviour observed during outdoor play in the less structured Oxford pre-school centres. These findings highlight a potential difficulty with readiness perspectives. They may dichotomize physical and cognitive learning, and leave unrealized the opportunities for challenging learning across the curriculum outdoors. Additionally, a number of studies indicate that any academic gains from an early and intense diet of direct instruction are likely to be short-lived (Frost et al. 2008).

The child explorer

Piaget's work, influential within early childhood education from the 1960s onwards, brings a very different perspective to thinking about learning and outdoor play. Piaget provides rich descriptions of children's perceptual and cognitive development, and he was the first researcher to provide a fully developed theory of stages of cognitive development (Parke 2004). His observations of his own children as babies challenged traditional views, leading to a new recognition of the competencies of young children. Although uninterested in applied issues himself, Piaget's work on play was highly influential and it led to educators claiming a central role for play in young children's cognitive development. Piagetian theory was particularly novel in constructing the young child as an independent explorer, and in identifying the child, not the adult, as the person to direct learning. Taking Piaget's perspective, the adult role becomes one of guide, observing and assessing in relation to stages of development, and then planning the physical and intellectual environment that will support children's active construction of knowledge and understanding (Raban et al. 2003). Piaget, like other theorists who claim that young children create knowledge by exploring the physical world, is termed a 'constructivist' (McNaughton and Williams 2009).

Piaget's work has influenced a number of early childhood education programmes, including an influential action-research project in an English nursery class with children from 2 to 5 years (Athey 2007). Athey worked as a teacher-researcher, implementing a programme to enhance the learning of inner-city children from disadvantaged families. The programme included an integrating focus on visits outside the nursery, including visits to a local park, a local police stable, and boat trips on the Thames. The adult role in this programme involved work with families, to jointly observe and record commonalities in children's behaviour, identified as schema. It also involved finely tuned interactions with children, to support their development through different levels of cognitive functioning, from motor action, through symbolic functioning, to thought. In this respect, Athey gives a significant role to adults in support of young children's cognitive development, departing from Piaget's original constructivist approach.

Outdoor play experience served an important role within this learning process, particularly at the level of motor action. For example, Athey (2007, p. 140) notes the children's fascination with spaces that contain and envelop, and she describes how children first explored this schema:

. . . project observations consisted of children either putting objects into containers or getting inside enveloping spaces – climbing in and out of enveloping spaces by various means, by steps and ladders, by crawling through, by levering themselves downwards into holes, and so on.

At this early stage of development, adults support children by maintaining a descriptive commentary on actions. Gradually, children take over the dialogue and begin to represent their experiences symbolically, for example through language, by drawing and painting, or through role-play. Over time, action schemas develop into higher-order concepts, often, as in the example below, supported by active outdoor experience:

Before Alistair (4: 6: 19) drew the tent . . . and said that there wasn't enough room inside for more children, he had systematically explored the tent in order to extend the schema of envelopment . . . His comments reveal a dawning awareness of the volume taken up by his own body in relation to the capacity of the tent. (Athey 2007, p. 146).

OBSERVATION POINT

Observe a group of toddlers or young children playing outdoors.

What repeated action patterns can you identify from the following?

- *Envelopment.*
  Children wrapping or covering themselves, other children or objects

- *Containment.*
  Children placing themselves or objects inside containing objects or structures.

What resources could you add to support this play?

Take note of:

- Examples of adults enriching children's action schema through talk.

- Examples of children representing the action schema through talk, mark-making or construction.

These and further examples (Meade and Cubey 2008) suggest ways in which adults, informed by cognitive developmental perspectives, can effectively support child explorers in outdoor learning environments. However, Frost et al. (2008) identify several critiques of Piaget's theory. Subsequent researchers have challenged Piaget's idea that children's learning is fixed within a particular stage and that children use domain-general learning mechanisms to develop concepts across all areas of development. Researchers such as Gelman and Brenneman (2004) have worked with pre-school teachers in the United States to develop early science and maths curricula, and argue that children approach new learning in ways that are domain-specific. For example, a child growing up on a farm may be precocious in understanding early scientific concepts relating to the natural world but have an understanding of number within expected norms. This research has implications for planning for children's learning during outdoor play. Gelman and Brenneman (2004) argue that young children need repeated experience over time of salient scientific concepts, for example the concept of living things.

REFLECTION POINT

Think of an early-years setting that you know well.

Reflect on the experiences provided for babies, toddlers or young children in the outdoor environment over their time in the setting.

- What living things are children interested in?

- What aspects of the environment support repeated experience of living things over a year or longer period?

- How do adults support children in gaining these experiences?

- How could practitioners enhance the environment and develop the adult role?

A nursery garden provides a valuable context for such experience as children can revisit outdoor experiences over time and through the different seasons. Gelman and Brenneman (2004) also recognize the need for an adult role in scaffolding early learning in this area. Like other researchers, they have challenged Piaget's focus on the child as a solitary explorer, as will be explained below.

An active partner in learning

Although Piaget recognized the importance of the social and the affective dimensions of learning (Siraj-Blatchford et al. 2002), this aspect was not the key focus of his theories. His work as a constructivist contrasts with social constructivist perspectives that recognize the importance of young children's interactions with their physical worlds, but theorize learning as primarily a social process. This emphasis on learning through social relationships can be found in the work of a range of researchers, including Bruner, Vygotsky, Schaffer and Bronfenbrenner. All emphasize the important learning that takes place in families and communities before formal school learning begins. Additionally, these theorists foreground the essential role of the adult or more competent child, who provides leadership and guidance to the child through interaction (Raban et al. 2003). Social constructivists foreground children's learning, including their playful learning, as they take on roles as social partners with adults and with more competent peers. Schaffer (1996) explains that this social role is evident from birth as infants participate in early social encounters around basic biological processes such as feeding and sleeping. From about two months of age, with much improved visual skills, infants become increasingly aware of other people, and social interaction develops around face-to-face encounters, including more prolonged gaze and social smiles. Until about five months, face-to-face interactions are the primary form of social engagement. From this point onwards, however, engagement with the world of objects becomes a focus for play, driven by the infant's increasing abilities to manipulate objects. Initially, at around six months, the child can attend to the object or the person. From about eight or nine months, however, an impressive range of new abilities emerges. The young child becomes able to co-ordinate a number of activities, for example turning attention between a carer's smiling face and a ball being rolled towards her on the grass. From this point, the child becomes an equal social partner in, for example, the adult–infant games such as Patacake and Peekaboo often played with this age group. Schaffer (1996) gives the term 'reciprocity' to the infant's new and significant achievement of active participation in such games. 'Intentionality' is a further social achievement at this time, seen in the game of ball, as the young child repeatedly gestures towards the ball, indicating that he or she would like the game to be repeated. Adults have an important role to play in supporting these emergent social skills. Schaffer (1996) explains how distinctive patterns of adult–child interaction are shaped by cultural influences, by the personalities of care-givers and also by the characteristics of each child as a unique person.

Scaffolding is a metaphor that has been used to explain how effective adult–child or peer interaction provides support for a child's learning. Attentive adults scaffold children's learning in the examples of adult–infant games, as noted above. Scaffolding is an approach to interaction that enables the child to perform at a level beyond his or her independent capability but within what is termed the 'zone of proximal development' (ZPD). The ZPD is the level of functioning that young children can work within, given adult or peer support.

In their guidelines for practitioners on the use of scaffolding, McNaughton and Williams (2009) propose distinct phases of involvement. First, practitioners should observe a child carefully, taking note of his or her cognitive, communicative and social competencies. In particular, they need to be alert to when a child is ready to move forward in learning, identifying what the next step might be. Following this, the practitioner should spend time with the child, individually or in a small group, interacting in ways that can support the child's progress. Parents and carers who have developed attachment relationships (Smith et al. 2003) with their children from birth often support learning more instinctively than practitioners who are working with a diverse group of young children. McNaughton and Williams (2009) suggest a range of relevant teaching techniques for practitioners to draw on when scaffolding children's learning, including questioning, confirming and modelling.

As explained above, the concept of scaffolding is relevant to work with the youngest children, and scaffolding can be used effectively during play episodes outdoors. Rayna's (2004) comparative study of professional practice in French and Japanese day-care centres provides an interesting account of two culturally distinct approaches to the education and care of children under the age of 1 year. In the Japanese centres, educators worked in a sustained and playful way to scaffold learning for the under-1s through adult–child interactions. Their practice reflected staff training and guidelines, which include a strong focus on how to play with young children, including babies. Play in the open air, in a garden or terrace, is also considered to be an important aspect of good practice and linked to the value that Japanese educators place on natural environments, social interaction and good health. The Japanese educators interacted intensively with the under-1s during extensive periods of play, which included adult-initiated songs, invitations to play with carefully selected objects, and the encouragement of physical play. Staff also gave time to supporting the children in participating in social play with peers and older children. This practice appears to include the key elements of scaffolding with babies (McNaughton and Williams 2009). Rayna's (2004) account suggests that the Japanese educators were concerned to identify a shared focus of interest, to establish joint interest in this focus, to demonstrate warmth and responsiveness, to hold a child within the ZPD, and to encourage each child to have control of his or her own learning.

Turning to work with pre-school children, the REPEY study of effective pedagogy in early childhood settings (Siraj-Blatchford et al. 2002) provides some examples of scaffolding where skilled practitioners facilitated episodes of 'sustained shared thinking' around what were often child-initiated interests and themes. In one successful outdoor activity, practitioners talked with children over an extended period, as they closely observed and drew slugs and snails. The practitioners modelled language, extended children's vocabulary, and shared their detailed knowledge of the animals. Where interaction of this quality occurs regularly, settings are particularly effective in promoting cognitive development. However, the REPEY study (Siraj-Blatchford et al. 2002) highlights the low frequency of such episodes in most settings.

The Japanese and REPEY examples suggest that outdoor environments can provide rich stimuli for playful talk and learning. However, it seems there is a need for settings to review the opportunities for adults to interact with children during play and to support episodes of scaffolding, including 'sustained shared thinking' outdoors.

Diverse childhoods

A fifth perspective considered by Raban et al. (2003) is that of critical theory. Critical social psychology highlights the multiplicity of views of childhood and expectations of children that exist within society. It questions any notion of a 'normal approach' to working with children and challenges practitioners to review taken-for-granted practices within their own culture. Rayna's (2004, p. 46) study of Japanese and French day-care centres demonstrates the value of comparative analysis for 'decentring from one's own point of view, for helping practitioners become aware of tensions within their beliefs and practices'. This is particularly important for the many practitioners who work within culturally diverse communities.

While Rayna's study compared cultural practices across two very different societies, Brooker's (2005) ethnographic study of a reception class in England brings to light the complex issues for the education of young children that relate to cultural diversity within one community. The teaching staff in Brooker's study held an idealized concept of the 4- and 5-year-olds in their reception class which assumed a natural ability to 'learn through play and exploration' (Brooker 2005, p. 118). However, most Bangladeshi families with children in this class had very different cultural expectations and views about children's learning. These significant differences in beliefs and practices relating to children, play and learning had negative consequences for several of the children from the Bangladeshi families as they started out on their school careers. While play provision was a key feature of the learning environment in Brooker's (2005) study, outdoor play opportunities as an integral part of the planned curriculum were not described. However, Brooker's (2005) call for a critical review of much current practice relating to a pedagogy of play is pertinent to our thinking about outdoor play. Brooker identifies a need for practitioners to examine critically their assumptions about play, to question the common work/play dichotomy in early-years curricula, to review the value placed on relationships as a key element of children's learning, to prioritize opportunities for peer learning, and to enter into a genuine dialogue with parents from diverse communities.

Raban et al.'s (2003) account of critical theory similarly highlights how a critical perspective leads to questioning of the individualistic focus of earlier approaches in psychology. Rather than viewing children as isolated beings, critical theory recognizes children as members of families and other groups within evolving communities. Brooker's study of a reception class evidences very clearly the complex social world of young children as they work to develop identities within very different home and school communities. Raban et al. (2003) suggest that practitioners should acknowledge children's relationships with diverse groups within the wider community, and aim to educate children in partnership with others.

In thinking through the implications of this perspective for outdoor play, there seems to be potential in working to engage families and the wider community in developing early-years outdoor environments in culturally relevant ways. Some settings, for example some children's centres in the UK, will have opportunities to develop outdoor areas in partnership with community groups and make these available for wider use. Additionally, there may be individuals and groups with a special contribution to make outdoors, for example groups with artistic, craft or gardening skills. Exemplifying this approach, Learning through Landscapes (2003) describes how one London primary school, serving a culturally diverse community, collaborated with families to develop a very special garden. Families shared knowledge of plants from a wide range of countries of birth, contributing to an environment that could be enjoyed by diverse community members.

Further examples of community gardens are the two case-study gardens in London, examined by Rishbeth (2004), which showed contrasting approaches to representing ethnic diversity. Both gardens were fairly small and located in densely populated areas. Chumleigh Gardens had small areas representing African, Islamic, Mediterranean and Oriental gardens, while Calthorpe Project used a range of strategies to involve community members from different ethnic groups. In general, residents from a range of ethnic backgrounds enjoyed the gardens as quiet havens in densely populated urban environments. However, Rishbeth's (2004) study identified differences among ethnic groups in response to the gardens. It also raised complex issues as to how best 'to empower people from all ethnic backgrounds to take a full role in shaping the built environment' (Rishbeth 2004, p. 331). The engagement of community members in gardening activities led by multi-ethnic staff was a successful aspect of the Calthorpe Project. In addition, the provision of food was also important in engaging community members, particularly members from cultures where eating outdoors is customary. The study has relevance for early-years settings that seek to involve ethnically diverse communities in the development of outdoor spaces for children and other community members to use.

Geographical perspectives

Wild places

Our sense of places that are special to us, both positive and negative, is an essential part of who we are. This includes the remembered places of childhood. Geographical perspectives on children and childhood have focused on understanding children's developing sense of place. Several studies highlight the importance of wild places for children (Wake 2007). For example, Nabhan (1994a, p. 7), drawing on observations of his own children, identifies the important emotional experience of comfort and intimacy that children can find in nature. Describing his daughter's excitement at her den built under the low spread of a hackberry tree, he notes:

> Over time I've come to realise that a few intimate places mean more to my children, and to others, than all the glorious panoramas I could ever show them. Because I sense their comfort there, their tiny hand-shaped shelter has come to epitomise true intimacy for me.

Trimble (1994, p. 24), reflecting on his own childhood, remembers the importance of natural objects, the collections of 'rocks, bugs, feathers, bones' that are the treasures of early childhood. He suggests that the experience of collecting enables children to develop a relationship with the Earth, gaining a sense of security and worth.

Geographical perspectives have implications for the development of outdoor environments and play. They remind us that children need wild areas to support emotional well-being and nourish a relationship with nature. In England, emotional well-being is an important aspect of 'Be Healthy' outcomes within the *Every Child Matters* (DfES 2004) framework, and this concept is recognized as significant in other early-years curricula internationally. Wake (2007, p. 31), reviewing research in this area, reports that positive childhood

REFLECTION POINT

Did you make collections as a child?

Did you make collections of natural objects?

What did you collect?

Think of some ways to encourage young children to make natural collections outdoors.

Starting points:

• Find some natural-world objects to fit in a tiny box.

• Find autumn leaves that match the colours on a section of a paint chart.

experience of nature has been linked to what is termed 'environmental sensitivity' and this may contribute to a sense of environmental responsibility. However, there are some children, growing up in urban environments, who now feel apathy or even fear in response to wild places. This trend may have negative, longer-term consequences for environmental citizenship. In response to such concerns, a children's garden movement has developed over the last two decades in the United States. While the aims and purposes are diverse, many gardens aim to provide urban children with opportunities to learn through playful and exploratory interactions with nature. Building on this tradition, Wake (2007) developed an evaluation and design tool for children's gardens, which she used in the design of the Potter Children's Garden (PCG) in Auckland, New Zealand. This is a garden for children to visit, closely linked to the New Zealand cultural and ecological context. However, it offers ideas for interactive experiences to inform planning of early-years gardens for young children to enjoy on a daily basis. PCG is designed as a journey through different kinds of ecological environments, but with an emphasis on native trees and plants that will attract wildlife. There are alternative pathways through the landscape, including stepping-stones and tunnels that allow children to make choices and to experience the unexpected. In one case, a tunnel is made from native tree-fern logs. There are sculptures and carvings representing Maori myths.

Gardens that relate to the stories of our cultures and the natural landscapes that are closest to where our early-years settings are located can provide opportunities for young children to experience the special qualities of natural places and things as described by Nabhan (1994a) and Trimble (1994). However, while garden design is important, Wake (2007) also emphasizes the importance of carer-givers who can interact with children to engage their interest in particular aspects of the garden and respond in a knowledgeable way to their questions.

Sociological perspectives

Children's peer cultures

Sociological perspectives also highlight the outdoors as a special place for young children's play, but emphasize the social purposes of play. Researchers identify outdoor areas as key physical and social spaces, within which children create their own peer cultures.

Corsaro (2005, pp. 1–2) vividly describes a scene in the outside play area of an Italian pre-school where children enjoy their unique creation, 'a travelling bank':

At some distance I saw three children marching around the yard carrying a large, red milk carton . . . There was a bucket inside the carton and it was filled with rocks.

'La barca?' I asked Antonio.

'No, la banca con soldi! (The bank with money!)' he said as he cupped his hand in a familiar Italian gesture.

I was intrigued. These kids had created a whole new dimension in banking, a bank that makes house calls!

Discussing the episode, Corsaro explains how young children commonly draw on ideas and experiences from the adult world in play but often recreate these in unique and surprising ways.

As well as dealing with adult themes, children's peer cultures and play address their particular concerns as children. Drawing on observations of children playing in American and Italian pre-schools, Corsaro (2005) suggests that children aged from 3 to 6 are intensely concerned with two themes. The first theme is that of social participation, for example establishing and sustaining shared play. Corsaro uses several examples of outdoor play to detail the strategies and rituals that young children use to enter and sustain shared play episodes. The second concern is with challenging and gaining control over adult authority, for example evading adult rules.

OBSERVATION POINT

Observe children's social play outdoors.

What strategies do toddlers and/or young children use to join groups of children who are playing?

What strategies do toddlers and/or young children use to sustain episodes of play?

Perry's (2001) ethnographic study of yard play in an American nursery builds on the ideas of Corsaro. She examines the outdoor fantasy play of 4- and 5-year-olds and argues that spontaneous and child-directed fantasy play outdoors is significant for young children's social and emotional development. Children's collaborative learning is highlighted; children learn what it means to be a friend and how to take on the perspectives of others through the process of play. Although she identifies making friends as a natural process, Perry highlights an important role for the early-years practitioner in supporting this. She documents the teachers' observations of the evolving peer cultures outdoors and explains how observations inform skilled and supportive interventions in play.

Connolly (1998) examines the social worlds of 5- and 6-year-olds, in an English, multi-ethnic inner-city primary school. Although focused on the hidden curriculum of school playtime, rather than an explicit pre-school curriculum, this study has wider relevance and challenges practitioners to look more closely at issues of gender and racism in the lives of young children. Emphasizing young children's social competency, Connolly (1998, p. 2) explores 'the complex ways in which racism intervenes in young children's lives and comes to shape their gender identities' within a peer culture. This important study (Connolly 1998, p. 195) challenges 'traditional notions of childhood innocence' and offers support to practitioners as they develop multicultural and anti-racist strategies.

These studies highlight the complexity of children's peer cultures and the importance of themes of friendship, gender and ethnicity. In England the *Every Child Matters* framework (DfES 2004) recognizes the need for adults to support 'Making a Positive Contribution' outcomes, which includes positive peer relations, in proactive ways. Taken together with the studies discussed above, this suggests a need for practitioners to observe very closely during outdoor play and, like Perry's (2001) skilled practitioners, use observations sensitively, to inform interventions that can promote social and emotional development.

Playwork perspectives

Over recent decades in the UK, playwork has developed as a distinctive approach to the play of children and young people, with playworkers representing a relatively new and distinct professional group. In England and Wales, the Children's Plan is shaping reconfigured children's services and recognizing the important contribution of play services to children's lives. Playwork has sometimes been defined by the kinds of contexts in which playworkers are employed, for example community and adventure playgrounds. Playworkers have traditionally worked in the places where school-age children *choose* to go, and not in the places that they *have* to go, for example schools. However, the boundaries between spaces for education, care and recreation are becoming blurred. In England, playworkers can be found working with children from 4 years of age, in the day-care provision of extended schools, and also in private and community nurseries. The playwork role has similarities with the role of pedagogues in parts of Europe, professionals who support the notion of 'upbringing' (Moss and Haydon 2008). Playwork is a wider concept than education as generally conceived, and it includes a concern for nurturing all aspects of the child's development, with a particular focus on personal, social and emotional development, and creativity. In England, a playwork approach fits well with the holistic approach of the *Every Child Matters* (DfES 2004) agenda. Playworkers value play in childhood as a part of children's lives but not as a vehicle to support children's development towards pre-defined learning goals.

Rather than thinking of playwork as a distinct profession, however, it can be useful to consider it as a philosophical approach to children's play that stands in a different tradition from educational approaches. Playwork raises questions in relation to dominant discourses of play in education and care settings for young children, particularly in countries where practice is shaped by prescribed learning goals.

This chapter has identified diverse theoretical perspectives on young children's development to inform practice around outdoor play. It has evidenced ways in which outdoor play can enrich children's lives. However, there are recurring and often complex issues that arise for practitioners who aspire to develop outdoor play as an essential curriculum strand. Gender differences, for example in children's use of outdoor play space, present difficult issues, while balancing safety and challenge in outdoor play is a further concern. These and other issues will be considered in the next chapter.

Further Reading

Meade, A. and Cubey, P. (2008), *Thinking Children: Learning About Schemas*. Maidenhead, Berkshire: Open University.

Perry, J. (2001), *Outdoor Play: Teaching Strategies with Young Children*. New York: Teachers College Press.

4 | Outdoor play decisions

> . . . it is often through discussion with someone who holds a
> conflicting point of view, that we are able to clarify our thinking
> and reach new insights. (Edgington 1998, pp. 201–2)

Practitioners who aim to work towards quality in outdoor provision
have to make some important decisions about principles and practice. This chapter uses nine outdoor stories to introduce some key
and recurring themes for discussion and decision-making. The
outdoor play themes to be examined concern:

- the relationship between the quality of outdoor play and programme structure;
- issues relating to the adult role in supporting young children's
  relationships during play;
- problems arising from diverse weather conditions;
- balancing the positive and negative aspects of messy play outdoors;
- resolving gender issues relating to space and styles of play;
- planning an inclusive outdoor learning environment;
- meeting children's need for physical challenge.

In exploring each of these areas, it is important to recognize that
team members may hold diverse views. It is also important to
acknowledge the diversity of early childhood settings; this militates
against universal solutions to problems. McNaughton (2000), consid-
ering the relevance of concepts from post-structuralism for improving early-years practice, suggests the value of standing back from
our taken-for-granted assumptions. Early-years teams work in
diverse cultural contexts, and team members may have diverse
perspectives. Consequently there are no prescriptive answers to the
issues that arise in particular settings. Each staff team will need to

explore the outdoor play issues independently, working towards shared viewpoints. In many settings, it will be important to access the perspectives of children, parents, carers and communities to support policy development. This section introduces the nine outdoor stories, presents research relevant to the issues raised and explores potential responses.

Programme structure

Outdoor story

Indoors–outdoors: children's choices
Groups at Willow pre-school had a chance to play out each day, and today it was the turn of the Red Room first. Reena watched and helped as her group of 3- and 4-year-olds rushed to be first with their coats and jackets.

It was a dull autumn day but the children were soon busily engaged outdoors. Several were keen to join the movement activity. Lively music accompanied them as they twisted and turned, making patterns in the air with brightly coloured streamers. Reena joined in the dance, praising and encouraging children as they moved to the music. She also encouraged turn-taking, so that all children could enjoy the streamers.

Just one child, Maya, hung back. Maya stood very still, observing other children as they played at the sand tray, built with wooden blocks, and made chalk patterns on the ground. Her face was impassive and she did not move until the half-hour had ended. Reena announced that it was time to change groups, and Maya's face brightened. She moved straight to the door and was first in the queue. She was keen to return to her home-corner play of the previous day. Amadur, however, was less enthusiastic. He had just filled his trolley with crates and was about to start transporting crates to the garage at the end of the path. This was not a good time to go in!

Later, at the weekly staff meeting, Reena shared her observations of Maya and Amadur. She felt that Maya was gaining little from outdoor sessions. She reminded the team of her visit to Maya and her mum at home, prior to admission to nursery. Living on the sixth floor of a tower block with her mum and a new baby, she felt that Maya probably had little experience of outdoor play. At the same time, Reena felt that the battle to persuade Amadur to comply with coming-in routines was exhausting for all. Reena was also concerned by Amadur's low-level play indoors, where he showed nothing of the concentration and persistence observed outside.

Reena's more experienced colleagues disagreed with her analysis. They argued that Maya had an entitlement to outdoor play, suggesting that any reluctance to play outdoors was normal for a new child and likely to be temporary. They were equally insistent that the programme structure was beneficial for Amadur, helping him conform to routines and take turns in his play.

The practitioner response: what would you do?
Some early childhood settings offer set periods of outdoor play, lasting from half an hour to an hour each session, providing each child with daily experience outdoors. During these periods, all children or a specified group play outdoors. In some settings practitioners choose this as their preferred approach, while in other settings it is prescribed by the limitations of buildings and staffing. Other early-years settings offer opportunities for more extended periods of indoor and outdoor play, with children moving independently between indoor and outdoor provision. These are important differences in programme structure.

Window on research

The Oxford Pre-school Research Project (Sylva et al. 1980) compared the experiences of children in Oxford and Miami pre-schools and identified significant issues relating to programme structure. It seems that children who are free to begin and end activities independently, as in the Oxford pre-schools, are more likely to engage in the extended bouts of play that are associated with cognitive complexity. Amadur's transporting and garage play represents play of high cognitive challenge, as identified by the Oxford Pre-school Research Project. It is therefore important to consider whether a stop–start schedule that cuts across such play places limits on children's learning.

Laevers' (2000) research is also relevant to the issues raised. His 'experiential' approach to early education and care identifies young children's 'emotional well-being' and levels of 'involvement' as key indicators of quality. Laevers uses the term 'experiential' to identify a programme that focuses on the moment-by-moment experiences of the child. He argues that emotional well-being and involvement underpin deep-level learning and are key concepts for practitioners working to improve the quality of their practice. Structures that lack flexibility may impede this process. For example, at this stage in her transition into the setting, group outdoor play was probably unhelpful for Maya. Adult support, encouraging co-operative play with new friends in the home corner, would have met her needs more effectively. In contrast, Amadur would have benefited, in terms of well-being and involvement, from adult support for ongoing play outdoors.

A final point concerns links between indoor and outdoor learning. Sylva et al. (1980, p. 60) suggest that play of high cognitive challenge includes play that is 'cognitively complex, involving the combination of several elements, materials, actions or ideas'.

Where practitioners encourage children to link indoor and outdoor themes and experiences, levels of cognitive challenge may be increased. A practitioner, supporting the play of Maya and her new friends in the home corner, might suggest a picnic in the garden with the babies to encourage this more complex play. Supported by the adult, the play could start off in the home corner, getting baby, picnic and picnic blanket ready for the outing, before moving outdoors onto the grass. This would allow Maya to have a positive early experience of outdoor play in the company of new friends, with adult support and within the safe boundaries of a self-selected play theme. It would also support the development of more complex role-play themes. This is one of many possibilities for linking indoor and outdoor play experiences.

For managers and lead practitioners dealing with staffing rotas and concerned to meet adult–child ratios, a fixed period approach to programme structure is attractive. A flexible approach requires more complex arrangements, with staffing attuned to the flow of children's interests. However, it is important for teams to review the extent to which fixed scheduling is supporting children's 'emotional well-being' and 'involvement'. It is also important to review the opportunities for children to connect actions and ideas into more complex play sequences. These opportunities may be very limited, particularly in small and crowded group rooms. Where teams decide to make changes to their programme structure, it is helpful to use an action research approach to change. This approach is described very clearly by Anning and Edwards (2006) in an account of several early-years action research projects. McNaughton and Hughes (2009) provide more detailed guidance on working through the action research process, again with a focus on early-years practice.

1- and 2-year-old quarrels: managing conflict

Outdoor story

Squabbles, squeals and making up
It was a bright and warm autumn day and all the children had arrived at Robins Room at Sunshine Nursery, a day-care setting for children from six months to 5 years. Lina, the senior practitioner, and Annette had opened up the French windows to their outdoor play space, and their group of 2-year-olds was soon outside, playing happily. The Robins group shared a play space with the younger children from the Ducklings Room. Maria, a practitioner in Ducklings, was also outside trying to settle George, a new child of just eight months. George was crying intermittently after his mum's departure, and Maria was speaking softly to him and trying to draw his attention to a sparkling mobile that glittered in the morning sun. George calmed quickly and became absorbed in Maria's game of shaking the mobile.

Outdoors, the children were playing happily, when Annette, as Harika's key person (Elfer et al. 2003) went back indoors with Harika to deal with a grazed knee. This was the result of Harika tumbling on the path when climbing off her trike. Kazuo and Aiden were digging with assorted containers and scoops in the expansive sand tray; Tori was feeding her teddy in the play cube, watched by Li Mei, who was crawling in through the attached tunnel; and Leroy was watering the newly planted apple tree, as well as himself! Meanwhile, Lina was sitting on the edge of the sand tray, talking with

Kazuo and Aiden about their filling and emptying activities while monitoring the wider area.

When Annette came back she immediately heard loud cries coming from inside the play cube. She was at first surprised and then cross to see that Lina was not going to investigate. Annette went quickly over to the play cube herself and found the two girls both pulling hard on the teddy, with the feeding cup on the ground. Lina assumed that Li Mei had the teddy first and firmly told Tori to come out and join the play with the boys in the sand tray. Tori came out reluctantly and held Lina's hand, walking over to the sand.

Later, when the children were sleeping, Annette asked Lina why she had not left the boys who were playing happily and gone over to sort out the quarrel. Lina explained that she was aware of what was happening and was monitoring the play. However, she had judged that the girls could sort out the quarrel for themselves. Her previous experience was that the two girls usually arrived at some kind of compromise, with conflict rarely escalating into a crisis. In addition, she felt that she was making good progress in supporting the peer play of Kazuo and Aiden, two boys who usually preferred play with an adult, and she had not wanted to interrupt this scaffolding.

The practitioner response: what would you do?

Window on research

Rayna's (2004) comparative study of professional practice in French and Japanese day care, described earlier, makes clear that there are differences in the ways in which practitioners from different cultures are likely to respond when babies are crying. It is to be expected that there would be similar differences in response to the play of slightly older children. Observing French practice, Rayna (2004) notes that caregivers did not hurry to provide comfort, although they did not leave babies crying for any length of time. However, observing this unfamiliar practice, Japanese educators were impressed by the ability of the French babies to play independently, an apparent outcome of these more detached relationships.

Turning to slightly older children, Singer (2002) has some pertinent conclusions about the abilities of 2- and 3-year-olds to deal independently with conflict among peers. Singer studied videotaped data of peer conflicts during the free play of 2- and 3-year-olds in one Finnish and nine Dutch day-care settings. She noted that most conflicts arose during joint or parallel play and that children showed a range of non-verbal strategies to ensure that disagreements rarely escalated into conflicts. The data suggest that practitioners may be no better at resolving conflicts than children themselves. Children were more likely to be separated when adults intervened, while, without intervention, children were more likely to continue playing together. Adults who 'resorted to higher power strategies' (Singer 2002, p. 62) as in half the adult interventions, unintentionally reinforced the power of one of the children. Such strategies included enforcing a solution, as in our outdoor story, blaming the child who appeared to be in the wrong, and supporting the apparent victim.

Singer (2002) suggests that practitioners do need to intervene when there is evidence of bullying behaviour and children are hurting each other to get what they want. However, in general she suggests a need for practitioners to strengthen children's pro-social behaviours, in part by recognizing conflict as a natural part of social life and ensuring that opportunities are provided for children to resolve conflict independently. Other proposed strategies include suggesting verbal tools for children to use in conflict situations, such as 'Take turns' and 'Don't hurt'; and helping children to verbalize feelings and activity ideas. Where adults feel they need to intervene, Singer suggests that they should try to respect the intentions of all children, and help to mediate, ensuring that the play continues.

This research suggests that peer conflicts are an expected part of the social world of young children playing together in group care settings. However, babies and toddlers appear motivated to invest in positive social relationships from early on. There is an important role for adults in promoting positive peer relationships but it requires a special kind of sensitivity to peer cultures. Observing young children's relationships in action may be a useful starting point for building practitioner skills in this area.

Unpredictable weather

Outdoor story

A place in which to play whatever the weather

Gerrard was looking forward to his day outside. It was one of the real positives of the job that at least once a week he could work with children in Mayville Nursery School's outdoor area. His enjoyment of outdoor play was one of the reasons he had chosen to specialize in early-years education at college.

The sky was blue as Gerrard and the team began setting up the attractive and diverse outdoor environment. The focus for the session was a mini-beast hunt. It had been planned after adults had observed the fascination of Naima and Charlene with worms, discovered in the digging patch a few days previously. Charlene had recently started at nursery and this was the first time staff had seen her absorbed in anything but home-corner play. Gerrard had organized resources to support the activity, with magnifiers, picture reference books and mark-making materials ready for use. However, by the time the children had self-registered, the sky had changed. Black clouds threatened overhead and the air felt chill. Gerrard was unsure what to do but quickly decided that an optimistic stance was required. He checked that jackets were buttoned and zipped, and then gathered a group around him on the logs to see what he had in his special box. The children, including Charlene, were enthralled as Gerrard introduced the menagerie of plastic spiders, beetles, caterpillars and bees. They joined in with his mini-beast rhymes, before enthusiastically taking up his challenge to set out on a real mini-beast hunt. The first group was a great success. At the end of the hunt, with raindrops beginning to fall, Gerrard encouraged several of the group to take the mark-making materials inside, to draw what they had found.

However, as he gathered together a second group which Naima excitedly joined, the driving rain began. All thoughts of mini-beasts were put to one side as Gerrard set to work to bring necessary resources under the canopy or back into the shed. The rest of the day was a frustrating one for Gerrard and the children. The weather was changeable, a few more attempts at a mini-beast hunt were rained off and, by early afternoon, the grassy area was unpleasantly muddy.

At the next staff meeting, Gerrard shared his frustration with the team. This led to heated discussion as to the value of planning for outdoor play when the weather was so unpredictable. One member of staff, Sylvia, seriously questioned the value and appropriateness of persisting with outdoor play in unreliable weather.

The practitioner response: what would you do?
Where practitioners work in climates with fast-changing weather conditions, planning for outdoor play will need to be flexible. The weather can be frustratingly unpredictable, with many changes in a single day, as Gerrard experienced. However, the overall pattern is predictable. Most settings can expect there to be hot and sunny days, wild and windy days, as well as grey and rainy days on many occasions throughout the year. In addition, many settings can anticipate at least one cold and snowy day each year, while for others this may be a more regular occurrence. Children are often interested or excited by the weather, as well as by other surprising outdoor events, and children's interests are an important starting point for learning. For example, where a garden includes a giant, purple buddleia in flower, sightings of butterflies are likely. The first sighting, however, will be a surprise and it is likely to arouse much interest.

The natural world is changeable and often unpredictable. It is these aspects of natural world events that are rich in potential for learning of all kinds, particularly early scientific learning.

Window on research

Woolley (2008), a landscape architect, reminds us that 'playing out in different weathers means that children learn about the elements such as wind and rain – or air and water' and that these can be linked to other kinds of learning about the natural world. Therefore, practitioners should be well prepared to exploit natural world events of this kind.

Understanding of scientific concepts can develop rapidly in the pre-school and early school years, where children have rich opportunities for first-hand experience, alongside adult talk and scaffolding (Gelman and Brenneman 2004). Keil (in Meadows 1993), for example, discusses the case of a 5-year-old who believed that rocks are alive. The child argued that rocks can have babies, evidenced in pebbles; rocks can grow, perhaps into larger rocks; and rocks can die, evidenced by their lack of movement. Meadows (1993) concludes that it is children's limited experience that is the key factor leading to errors of this kind. Building on this research, Gelman and Brenneman argue that, if young children are to achieve understanding of concepts such as the animate–inanimate distinction at issue in the story above, they need extended periods of time and repeated experiences, supported by adult scaffolding. Well-planned outdoor play can offer these experiences.

Responsive teaching in outdoor environments is most likely to happen where adults are well prepared to exploit exciting but unpredictable events. Ouvry (2000) and Edgington (2002) present ideas for planning that build on children's natural enthusiasm for windy and rainy weather, as well as other events in the natural world. For example, practitioners can collect together sets of resources in boxes of varying sizes to be brought out in response to particular events, and particularly natural world events. The case study for short-term planning below includes suggestions for the kinds of resources that can be kept in readiness for a rainy day. Working in this way, Gerrard and his team might find that unpredictable weather became less of a problem, while offering new opportunities for enjoyable and stimulating learning.

All kinds of weather

Outdoor story

A blue-sky day

The staff at Swinburn College Nursery had recently moved into a new, purpose-built nursery, with a much enlarged outdoor area, and the new college term was about to begin. Nasreen, the Nursery Manager, was optimistic that, after years of struggle to provide outdoor play in a tiny, featureless yard, the new area would make outdoor play trouble-free. At the first staff meeting of the year, Nasreen explained that money left over from the new-build budget would be made available to each of the four group rooms to support further development of provision. However, she felt it would be wise to delay spending, to wait and see what outdoor play needs appeared over the first term. The team also discussed plans to increase outdoor play opportunities for all groups, including the two youngest groups in Tigers Unit, who shared a spacious outdoor area to the side of the nursery. They agreed, where possible, to encourage free movement for children between indoor and outdoor areas.

The new term began with clear, blue skies and two weeks of unexpectedly hot, sunny weather. Nasreen spent little time in the office over this period, instead spending time in each group room, assessing how new children were settling in and how the new building was working. There were some annoying problems with the new building, for example an intercom system that didn't work and high windows that no one could open. However, Nasreen was delighted at how well the indoor–outdoor flow of play was working in the two rooms for older children. In addition, children who were moving to new rooms and children starting at nursery for the first time had all settled more quickly than usual. However, whenever Nasreen went into Tigers Unit, she was disappointed to see all the youngest children indoors, and often several children crying.

Nasreen waited until her regular meeting with Abdul, the Unit Leader, to ask about the plans for extended outdoor play. Abdul explained that staff had agreed to keep the Tigers children inside because of the hot weather. The new area was far more exposed to the sun than the previous yard, where children could play in the shade cast by an established oak tree in the garden next door. Plantings in the new garden were all low-level and low-maintenance plants, and there were no taller plants to provide shade. In addition, several of the babies were very fair skinned and likely to get burnt. Staff had noticed children becoming tired and fractious during the first attempts to offer outdoor play in the new garden. Nasreen reminded Abdul about the nursery policy on outdoor play, but he remained unconvinced that this was appropriate in such hot weather.

The practitioner response: what would you do?

Window on research

Sun protection is an important issue for early-years settings. Boldermann et al. (2006) explain that 80 per cent to 90 per cent of skin cancers in Western societies are caused by exposure to ultraviolet (UV) radiation from the sun, particularly by exposure in childhood. Furthermore, babies need particular consideration because a baby's skin is five times thinner than adult skin. Therefore, Great Ormond Street Hospital (2009) recommends that under-1s stay out of strong sunlight and, on hot, sunny days, be kept in the shade. Other children who require particular protection from the sun are children with fair hair or skin, and children with a lot of moles or freckles.

Many early-years settings have outdoor areas that offer little protection from the sun. For example, Susan Herrington's (2008) study of the successful and unsuccessful features of outdoor play spaces at Canadian childcare centres identifies exposure to the sun as a negative feature of several settings. This includes settings with rooftop play spaces. She notes the increasing numbers of rooftop play spaces in Vancouver nurseries, a consequence of the high cost of land and the city's plans for densification. Such play spaces are particularly prone to the problems of heat and wind exposure.

A Swedish study (Boldermann et al. 2006) provides evidence of an important relationship between the qualities of outdoor environments and children's health during outdoor play in sunny weather. Boldermann et al. (2006) studied the play of

4- to 6-year-olds in the outdoor spaces of eight Swedish pre-schools. In three of these centres, children spent most of their time outdoors, including mealtimes. Outdoor environments were evaluated in a number of ways, including the size of play areas and the density of trees and shrubbery, particularly near play structures and play areas. The conclusion of the study was that spacious outdoor areas with trees and shrubbery provided protection from UV radiation and triggered higher levels of physical activity. However, in two pre-schools with sun-exposed environments, practitioners regularly kept children indoors on sunny days, leading to lower levels of physical activity.

Therefore, to promote 'Be healthy' outcomes (DfES 2004) for young children, practitioners and managers should review the use of trees and taller shrubs in their play space. This is a potential starting point for development work at Swinburn College Nursery.

Trees and plants can be used in a range of ways to increase areas of shade, while enhancing opportunities for different kinds of play and sensory experience. Wood and Yearley (2007) suggest ways to create secret hiding places with natural plantings, for example willow tunnels and weeping or overhanging trees such as weeping ash or silver birch. Pergolas and arches, covered in hardy climbing plants such as honeysuckle, can provide further attractive areas of dappled shade. Wooden shelters or playhouses, bought from equipment manufacturers or made by local builders, also offer shade as well as special places for imaginative play.

Moving to dens, a willow tepee, with woven walls made from a range of natural and manufactured material, makes an enticing and long-lasting den. Most nurseries will need professional support to build structures of this kind, although children can still be actively involved in their construction.

For more improvised and less permanent dens, outdoor den-building offers rich opportunities for playful learning, as well as providing welcome shade. For example, den-building can support the development of early knowledge, understanding and skills in both technology and science, while imaginative play is supported by

Illustration 4.1: A den in the woods

the private spaces offered by dens. Large cardboard boxes, which children can embellish in various ways, offer the simplest kinds of dens, while children and adults working together can build structures that are more complex. These can be made from a variety of materials, including hollow blocks, crates, large logs and old-fashioned clothes horses. Fabrics of different kinds can be draped over structures to create varied effects, from light, dappled shade to near darkness. Open fencing can be used as a part of the structure and fabrics fixed with a variety of fasteners, including large clothes-pegs and bulldog clips. For ready-made dens, tents of various sizes, particularly pop-up tents for ease of use, can offer shady places for particular activities. A nursery garden for under-2s might include a quiet storybook tent, a treasure basket tent and a role-play tea-party tent. Play tunnels and cubes, separate and joined together, offer further shady spaces, inviting more active play on sunny days. Jan White (2008) offers detailed suggestions for materials to use and the potential for learning and development of den-building and other kinds of construction play outdoors.

Further sources of shade are large parasols, both stand-alone or fixed to picnic tables, and children's umbrellas that offer shade on

Illustration 4.2: Painting a box

the move. Finally, when funding allows for more significant expenditure, a canopy structure fixed to the building offers protection from both sun and rain and an outdoor space for play in all weathers.

As well as providing varied opportunities for play in shady places, it is important to consider other approaches to sun protection. Great Ormond Street Hospital (2009) in England advises that children need to use sun block or sun lotion with a high sun protection factor (SPF), with a recommended level of between 30 and 60. In addition, 'broad spectrum' lotions are recommended, providing protection against UVA and also UVB light. Sun hats are important in sunny weather, and sun hats with wide brims or back flaps provide the most effective means of protecting children's necks and faces.

In all these activities, it is important to engage children and parents in learning about the need for protection from the sun. Older children who understand that the sun can burn their skin are more likely to take responsibility for putting on protective lotions and bringing sun hats to nursery. By acknowledging the dangers of the sun and planning for safe play outdoors, we can provide a more stimulating and attractive play environment, an environment that is inviting to children and adults in all sorts of weather.

Messy play

Outdoor story

Mixing the chocolate cake
It was a sunny spring afternoon and most of the children in the Brookfield Early Years Unit had chosen to play outdoors. Under the trees, a small group of girls had started to fill the shallow hollow of a tree stump, carrying soil by the handful from a nearby tractor tyre. With mounting excitement they collected twigs and sticks, added handfuls of mown grass and began to stir. Soon it was clear that this wasn't just a strange mixture on the improvised cooker, but a delicious 'chocolate cake'.

A younger boy, helping to fill the nearby water tray, came over with his bucket to see what was happening. He began to pour water slowly into the mixture, watching intently as it trickled onto the soil. The girls continued to poke and stir at the gooey and splattering chocolate cake but soon they were rushing off for fresh supplies. This time it was for 'sugar' from the dry sand tray on the other side of the playground.

At this point Kerry called to Miss Cohen to came and admire their cake. Miss Cohen was initially horrified to see the mud splattered on Kerry's white tee-shirt. Her mother would be furious. She was also aware that the cake was on the point of flowing out of the pan, onto the clothes of several other smartly dressed children. However, Miss Cohen also sensed the special qualities of the children's play and she was reluctant to cut across their intense pretend world.

The practitioner response: what would you do?
Child-directed play such as this rarely appears on adults' planning grids and can pose a range of problems. However, play of this kind may have a special quality of intensity not found in more adult-directed or conceived play contexts. The special quality of play in this case arises first from the child-led social context, with children working with shared engagement and a high level of co-operation.

Window on research

De Hann and Singer (2001) highlight the significance of child-led play contexts for children's learning about togetherness and friendship. Corsaro (2005) provides further insights into the distinctive features of young children's peer cultures and the importance of the theme of friendship within these.

The intensity of experience in this case also arises from children's engagement with an outdoor place, incorporating a diversity of natural, open-ended materials. Children, in this garden, play with soil, twigs, grass, leaves, stones and sand, incorporating these into a variety of play themes. Jan White (2008) offers a wide range of ideas for extending such creative play, taking account of the special value that young children place on diverse, natural places. She provides detailed suggestions for play on a variety of scales, using the following materials: sand and soil, wood in different forms, stones of various sizes, a range of plants and parts of plants, a variety of seeds, as well as shells, feathers and minerals.

Exploratory and imaginative play in such diverse environments contributes positively to young children's development. However, there is a need for practitioners to plan for the manageability of such play. Practitioners who value this play need to establish appropriate dress codes for children and adults. Informal, easy-to-clean clothing and readily available aprons all contribute to the manageability of messy play. In many cases practitioners will need to share views about the importance of such play with parents, carers, and, in some cases, school managers. In addition, children can be involved in discussing the issues that arise, perhaps outside the immediate play context. Children and adults together can develop rules to ensure the manageability of outdoor play. Children also need support to learn necessary practical and self-help skills, such as collecting and putting on aprons.

Gender

Outdoor story

Girls and boys come out to play
It had been warm and sunny for two days, providing the first chance for the 4- and 5-year-olds at Newlands Primary to play on the grass after weeks of rain. The grassy area by the apple tree had been set up with a climbing frame, as well as tyres, crates, ropes and planks for building. A group of the older boys raced into the garden as soon as the doors were pulled back, rushing past the home corner towards the building area. A saucepan toppled from the cooker as they passed by and crashed to the ground. A small group of girls, who had settled to play at house under the veranda, called after them with indignant voices, 'You've spilt our dinner! We're telling Mrs Khan now, we're telling her!' There was no reply.

The boys rushed headlong into the construction area, cheerfully unaware of the upset caused. Soon they were engrossed in play, collecting and transporting crates for their quickly growing police station.

Mrs Khan had observed the incident and heard the upset voices. Seeing Ellie rushing over to tell the tale, she was inclined to suggest that the girls continue with their play and ignore this as just a minor incident. However, she was also aware that incidents of this kind were a daily occurrence during outdoor play. She was unsure what to do.

The practitioner response: what would you do?
It is important for practitioners to discuss the complex and sometimes puzzling gender issues that occur regularly during outdoor play in early childhood settings. Research from a range of theoretical perspectives can inform reflective practice.

Window on research

Smith et al. (2003) outline psychological perspectives on gender that identify and theorize, first, early sex differences in behaviour and, second, developments in young children's own knowledge and understanding in this area. While boys and girls share many early interests, there is evidence of clear play preferences by the age of 3 and 4, preferences of the kind observed by Mrs Khan. Girls tend to choose home-corner play, dressing-up and play with dolls. In contrast, boys are likely to enjoy play that is more active, for example block play, play with balls, wheeled toys, and rough-and-tumble play. By 5 years, boys engage in more play-fighting than girls, and they are more likely to behave aggressively. Smith et al. (2003) review cross-cultural studies which suggest that such differences in behaviour are relatively stable across cultures. However, there is some evidence of differences that relate to different societal expectations of girls and boys.

Alongside differences in play choices, young children also demonstrate a growing awareness of gender identity. Children are likely to show some understanding of stereotypically male and female play choices from $2^1/_2$ years. By 4 years, most children can identify their own gender and that of others, as well as recognize gender as a stable aspect of identity.

As Mrs Khan's experience suggests, gender is a salient feature of young children's identity and of their social worlds. To address the issues raised in practice, it seems important to seek explanations for these gendered behaviours. Some researchers emphasize 'nature' or the biological factors that may pre-programme behaviours from early childhood onwards (Smith et al. 2003). In contrast, social learning theorists emphasize the role of 'nurture', in particular adult reinforcement of what is seen to be gender-appropriate behaviour.

Cognitive–developmental theorists ascribe a more active role to children in the socialization process and explain the process of learning to be a girl or a boy as rooted in children's cognitive development. They argue that gender schemas, developing from early childhood onwards, serve to focus children's observations of peers, guiding their imitations of gendered behaviours.

However, a single explanation of gendered differences in behaviour may be too simple. Maccoby's (in Smith et al. 2003) most recent research suggests that the development of early gendered behaviours is shaped by an interaction of biological, social learning and cognitive–developmental factors.

Cross-cultural studies evidence children's increasing preference for play and socialization with same-sex peers as they move through childhood (Smith et al. 2003). Maccoby (in Smith et al. 2003) highlights differences in the behaviours of these peer groups, with competition and risk-taking characteristic of male groups, and collaboration characteristic of female groups. She argues that children's involvement in same-sex peer groups contributes positively to the development of sexual identity.

The implications of this research for practitioners are complex. At Newlands Nursery, it may be important for children's development of sexual identities that practitioners support children's preferences for extended periods of play in same-sex groups. However, there may be problems in accepting uncritically the 'naturalness' of same-sex groups and gendered behaviours. Social learning theory highlights a role for adults in shaping gendered behaviours and this raises questions about the values of the wider society in relation to gender and equal opportunities.

Window on research

McNaughton (2000, p. 1), working within the framework of feminist post-structuralist theory, critically reviews what she describes as 'nine common myths about gender equity in early childhood', including some of the perspectives outlined above. She draws on research in Australian early childhood settings to highlight the potentially problematic features of same-sex peer groups and gendered behaviours. For example, she argues that during free play, boys regularly use physical power to control spaces, including girls' spaces. Although this seems to be part of learning what it means to be a boy, this kind of behaviour can have negative consequences for girls. The danger is that children and sometimes adults come to see outside spaces as boys' territory, while seeing particular resources, such as wheeled toys, as boys' toys. McNaughton (2000) suggests that practitioners should acknowledge gender as a category to support their observations of play. This is likely to lead to significant changes to the curriculum and to teaching styles, and she proposes a range of teaching strategies with relevance for the adult role during outdoor play. For example, practitioners should take a more interventionist approach during free play, establishing rules to support gender rights and challenging sexism during play. Taking account of children's agency, she also proposes that adults talk with children about gendered relationships during play and seek their understanding of specific incidents.

In responding to the incident above, it would be important for Mrs Khan to reassure the girls that their concerns were recognized. It would be helpful to discuss the issues with the children involved, encouraging recognition of the need for boys and girls to respect the play spaces of others. However, rather than interrupting the flow of play, it might be more appropriate to plan for a reflective discussion away from the incident, perhaps during a small group or circle time.

Window on research

In a large-scale study of early childhood settings, Siraj-Blatchford et al. (2002, p. 12) found that effective settings developed strategies that 'supported children in being assertive, at the same time as rationalising and talking through their conflicts'.

McNaughton and Williams (2009) suggest that, where practitioners introduce imaginative and human dimensions into play areas dominated by boys and where they model play, girls are likely to become enthusiastic players.

In responding to the incident above, Mrs Khan would need to respect children's preferences for play in same-sex peer groups for some of their time outdoors. However, she could consider developing outdoor play themes with appeal to both groups, introducing, for example, a canteen in the police station. Information books could be used to promote further discussion about workplace roles, and a widening of the roles children are confident to explore through play. Mrs Khan's active involvement in the play, perhaps in role as a police officer, could further encourage participation by the girls.

Finally, McNaughton and Williams (2009) advise that the process of changing gendered patterns of play is a complex one. Therefore, any strategies used will need to be monitored carefully for both intended and unintended consequences.

Inclusion

Outdoor story

A place in which to play – a place in which to grow strong
Jonathan works at Montague House, an integrated children's centre for children from 2 to 5 years, that has a high proportion of children considered to be 'at risk' of SEN in terms of delayed cognitive development and difficulties with social and emotional development. The centre includes a small number of children with statements relating to specific disabilities, including speech and language disorders and

physical disabilities. Jonathan is a senior teacher in the centre, with special responsibility for disabled children and children with SEN. He has recently taken on an additional responsibility for outdoor play, and the staff team has identified this as an area for development.

The centre has three connected playrooms, opening onto a spacious paved patio. There is a large, grassy area, pathways for wheeled toys, a chequerboard garden and plentiful resources. However, to date the centre has focused little attention on the needs of children 'at risk' of SEN or disabled children during outdoor play. Jonathan sees this as the starting point for development.

The practitioner response: what would you do?
Jonathan has made a positive decision to focus on outdoor play to support children with disabilities and 'at risk' of SEN.

Window on research

A Learning through Landscapes study of children and school grounds (Stoneham 1996) presents clear findings of the value of school grounds for children with SEN. It highlights the importance of outdoor environments for the development of physical skills, for building confidence, and for promoting social and behavioural skills. A more recent study (Sammons et al. 2003), focusing on children from 3 to 6, highlights the importance of high-quality provision in improving the cognitive and social behavioural development of vulnerable children. Provision in this study was assessed using ECERS-R (Harms et al. 1998), a rating scale that includes ratings of outdoor areas, as well as levels of adult supervision and interaction outdoors.

To develop outdoor play in this centre, Jonathan and his team should undertake a review of three key and interconnected areas. They should consider adaptations and enhancements of the environment; the selection and arrangement of resources; and the quality of interactions during outdoor play, including adult–child and child–child interactions.

Doctoroff (2001), discussing indoor environments, provides useful suggestions for adaptations that can maximize the participation of disabled children in play. Jonathan's team will find it helpful to arrange defined play areas with visible barriers, and to include some quiet zones, particularly for children who are over-stimulated by noisy play or who dislike noise. In addition, pathways on paved areas could be marked and pathways on grass widened to ensure accessibility for wheelchairs and walkers.

In selecting play materials, it is important to include resources matched to a diverse range of abilities across areas. For example, to promote motor skills it may be necessary to include three-wheeled scooters and pedal-less bikes among wheeled toys, while tactile and oval balls can be provided alongside traditional balls. Turning to role play, Doctoroff (2001) explains that children with cognitive delay are more likely to engage in pretend play if props, for example food and kitchen equipment, are highly realistic. However, non-realistic, open-ended materials can provide challenge and stimulate creative and imaginative play for children who are more advanced cognitively. Where children have significant motor impairments, materials will need to be adapted and assistive technology used. A source of more detailed information is provided in the final chapter of this book.

The Montague House team should also consider involving children in the development of wildlife areas. Trees, shrubs, flowers and bird feeding stations can be used to attract wildlife to the grounds. There is some evidence that such activities are particularly helpful for children with behavioural difficulties (Stoneham 1997). The team could also develop sensory features within the garden, involving colour, light, texture, smell and sound (Bishop 2001). Useful developments include a herb garden, an overgrown grassy area, mobiles, wind-chimes and the use of decorative tile or mirrored materials. Sensory experiences can contribute to cognitive and emotional development for a range of children (Stoneham 1997).

Doctoroff (2001) suggests that clear organization of resources is also important for children who have conditions such as Attention Deficit Hyperactivity Disorder (ADHD), where there may be difficulties in focusing and sustaining attention, as well as difficulties in regulating emotional responses. The Montague House team will need to ensure good organization and labelling of outdoor storage, for example using crates and shelving on wheels. Clear organization can help children to make play choices and to contribute to the maintenance of the environment. The placement of resources at appropriate levels is also important for children in wheelchairs. Where disabled children have visual disabilities, it is essential to place resources consistently, and to provide warnings and additional help where adults have made necessary changes to the environment.

The quality of interactions during outdoor play is the third key area for review, including both adult–child and peer interactions.

Window on research

The Early Years Transition and Special Educational Needs Project (Sammons et al. 2003) demonstrates a significant link between the quality of adult–child interaction and the progress of 'at risk' young children, in terms of cognitive and behavioural development.

The Montague House team could consider formalized evaluation and action planning to promote improvements in this area. Pascal and Bertram (1997), for example, evidence the impact of the Effective Early Learning Project as an approach to evaluation and action planning on levels of adult–child interaction in nursery settings, including interaction during outdoor play.

Peer interaction is a further area for review.

Window on research

Some studies (Hestenes and Carroll 2000) evidence relatively high levels of solitary play among disabled children and relatively low levels of play with typically developing peers. Some disabled children, for example children with autism, can have difficulties or delays in the area of social development (Doctoroff 2001).

In addition, children without disabilities may be wary of children who appear to be different in some way. Therefore, to promote positive social experiences for disabled children during outdoor play, adults need to be proactive. To foster positive peer relationships, Jonathan's team could begin by undertaking an audit of outdoor resources to promote social play. Balls, rocking toys, wagons, trolleys and tandem trikes are all useful resources, and outdoor role play, for example a garage or shop, offers further opportunities for social play. In addition, McNaughton and Williams (2009) suggest that adults should consider supporting peer play, for example through the use of social reinforcement techniques such as a hug for a child who engages with a disabled child in an appropriate way.

There is a range of strategies for enhancing outdoor play for disabled children and their peers to be considered by Jonathan and the Montague House team. The three key areas for review are adaptations and enhancements of the environment, the selection and arrangement of resources, and the quality of interactions.

Listening to children

Outdoor story

Baby Bears' voices – what do they say?
Jamila was a key person for five children who were under 2 in Snowdrops, the group room for the youngest children at The Three Bears Kindergarten. She had worked in early-years services for many years, brought up her own family, and now, at a relatively late stage in her career, she was working towards a degree. Jamila had always been a quiet but effective member of the team in the different nurseries where she had worked, but now, with the self-confidence that had grown with her studies, she was becoming more assertive about her own values as a practitioner. Although Jamila was very happy at The Three Bears, she was becoming increasingly impatient about what she perceived to be inequities in staff approaches to the different age groups. There seemed to be an implicit assumption, held by several staff, that working with the older children was a more challenging role, requiring more highly qualified practitioners. At times, there were also disparities in the resources given to different groups. For Jamila, matters had come to

a head over recent plans to develop the outdoor area, using a 'listening to children' approach.

Macy, the Deputy Manager, had recently attended a course on 'listening to children' and had come back to nursery with enthusiasm for how this approach could be used to gain children's perspectives on outdoor play. She felt that children's views, together with staff and parents' views, should be used together to inform the developments that were being planned. Macy had led a staff meeting where the team discussed how this approach could be put into practice over the coming six months. However, both Macy and Anja, the Baby Bears Room Leader, felt that the proposed approaches were inappropriate for the under-2s. Most children in the room were under 18 months and few children were talking in more than one- or two-word sentences. Jamilia felt intuitively that the senior staff members were wrong, but, in learning about 'listening to children' approaches at college, she had not read about any work with babies. However, she was confident that she could communicate with her key children well enough to understand their preferences. The difficulty was that she was not sure how to present her arguments at the second meeting to take place in a fortnight's time.

The practitioner response: what would you do?
There has been much written about children's participation over the last two decades, with evidence of an increasingly 'dominant discourse of voice and participation' (Clark et al. 2005, p. 2). Clark et al. (2005) argue that this participation discourse can be seen in a number of ways. There is a growing children's rights movement, exemplified by the United Nations Convention on the Rights of the Child, new approaches in sociology that increasingly recognize children as active participants forming a distinct social group, and economic changes that lead to children being acknowledged as consumers and customers. However, much work in this field has focused on children and young people. While there has been a growth in projects that seek to identify young children's perspectives on their preschool experience to inform developments of practice (Clark and Moss 2001; Clark 2007), work focused on the under-2s is more limited. It seems likely that the reason for this relates to the challenges of understanding the perspectives of pre-verbal children. There are, however, some positive examples of listening to the youngest children and some relevant guidance.

A set of six National Children's Bureau leaflets (National Children's Bureau 2008) provides guidance on approaches to listening. The leaflets summarize research, practice and methods that support this focus on children's perspectives. The set includes a leaflet on listening to babies (Rich 2008), which provides a definition of 'listening', with four components. The first component makes it clear that the process of listening is by no means dependent on spoken language, and it acknowledges diverse forms of communication. It is 'an active process of receiving, interpreting and responding to communication. It includes all senses and emotions and is not limited to the spoken word' (Rich 2008, p. 1). The leaflet defines 'young babies' as up to eight months, and 'babies' as from eight to eighteen months. Babies within this age range use crying for a variety of purposes, including communicating how they feel, and they use a variety of other sounds and body movements in communicative ways. Young babies also use gaze when interested in an object or event and they turn away when bored, giving further clues as to their interests. Rich (2008) suggests that adults who are committed to communicating with babies and who know them well, will understand how pre-verbal children feel and recognize their preferences.

Lancaster (2006), drawing on the experience of the Coram Family's Listening to Young Children Project, provides an example of how a video camera at a baby massage class was used to support an anxious first-time mother to tune in to her six-month-old baby boy. By playing the footage at slightly slower than normal speed, the mother became aware of the intensity of the child's feelings towards her during interaction. Lancaster (2006, p. 69) suggests that video can be particularly helpful in listening to 'babies, toddlers, children with disabilities, and children who do not have English as their first language'.

Jamila was confident in her abilities to listen to the children she knew well as their key person. Thinking about her children outdoors, Jamila knew that when Jack stopped crying and gazed intensely at the shiny, twirling spinner for several minutes, he was showing his special interest in such events. Similarly, Aloise, lying on the blanket under the shade of the trees, kicking her bare legs and gurgling, was showing pleasure in the opportunity for vigorous movement and perhaps the sensory experience of outdoor smells and dappled shade. As a further example, Jamila could remember the day when there was minimum staffing, and Nikhil, a usually content six-month-old baby, cried intermittently while sat with a basket of natural objects, showing little interest. She was sure that he was communicating a need for more personalized interaction and she knew that, without it, he would not enjoy the outdoor play.

Listening to babies is therefore to a large extent about tuning in to children's feelings in relation to their everyday experiences. The NCB leaflet (Rich 2008) also suggests that listening can be about a specific consultation. With babies, however, a consultation in relation to outdoor play would need to draw upon adult observations of children's outdoor experiences to inform any developments of practice. Practitioners could share their own observations of babies' responses to outdoor experiences with parents and carers, and ask for feedback on the baby's likes and dislikes when at home with family members.

Turning to an example of practice, Driscoll and Rudge (2005), as the Head of Centre and teacher at Fortune Park Children's Centre, describe the way they use 'profile books' as an approach to listening to children, including under-2s, involving both children and families. They explain how the books become a co-constructed representation of the child's 'life, interests, learning and development' (Driscoll and Rudge 2005, p. 91). In addition, they describe how special the books become for children, for example as a transitional object between home and centre. The books represent children's experiences in a variety of ways, for example through photographs, drawings and records of children's use of language, accurately recorded. Children learn that their voice is valued through the sharing of 'profile books' between children and between children and adults.

These approaches may be relevant to the work with under-2s at The Three Bears Kindergarten. By documenting the outdoor experiences of children under 2 and using 'profile books' to support shared reflection on experience, whether verbal or non-verbal, adults can begin to gain an understanding of young children's views. Our knowledge of what experiences children enjoy and find interesting, both at home and in the setting, can inform our developments of practice. For example, observation of Jack and the spinner suggests that an appropriate development for the Baby Bears garden would be to build a pergola over part of the patio, providing opportunities for a range of coloured and shiny spinners and mobiles. New trees would provide further opportunities for hanging mobiles of different sizes, attracting Jack's attention to a range of sounds. There are strong arguments for paying attention to babies' voices to inform effective developments of provision outdoors.

Health and safety

Outdoor story

Scarey, darey outdoor play

James was recently appointed as the team leader for the 3–5-year-old group in the High Trees Early Years Centre. In his previous setting there had been clear and detailed health and safety guidelines for outdoor play, and all staff followed these. In this new centre, however, James was becoming increasingly concerned about the inconsistency of staff practice and the divergence of views in relation to health and safety.

A particular issue for the centre was the play of 3- and 4-year-olds on the tall slide. While most staff reinforced the agreed rule of 'up the steps and down the slide', Carole, a new member of staff, was allowing children to climb up the slide, slide down head first and even hang from the edge of the slide. When asked to reinforce centre rules by a senior member of staff, Carole had defended her approach. She argued that the outdoor play area was lacking in opportunities for physical challenge, particularly for older children. She also argued that the children were well aware of their own abilities and unlikely to take risks. James understood and accepted some of these arguments. Nevertheless, he was clear that his own responsibility for health and safety in the centre was paramount. The situation was complex and he was unsure as to how to proceed.

The practitioner response: what would you do?

Quality assurance schemes for early-years settings present a consensus on the need to promote health and safety during outdoor play. The Early Childhood Environmental Rating Scale – Revised (Harms et al. 1998, p. 22), a tool used internationally for research and programme improvement, identifies 'adequate supervision to protect children's safety' as providing a minimal level of quality outdoors. At the 'excellent' level, 'play areas are arranged to avoid safety problems' and 'children generally follow safety rules'. Guidance of this kind is important in reminding practitioners of their significant responsibility for children's health and safety. It is important, however, to acknowledge that such criteria may be deceptively straightforward. While we may all agree on the need to arrange play areas 'to avoid safety problems' (Harms et al. 1998, p. 22), there may be less agreement concerning what counts as a problem.

Senda (1992), Japanese architect and designer of children's play environments, argues that contemporary societies have become over-protective of children in their concern for safety. As a consequence, increasingly children are deprived of physically challenging experiences, kept 'enclosed in a cage called safety' (Senda 1992, p. 5). Senda's innovative play environments, including outdoor play structures for young children, are designed to provide opportunities for real physical challenge. Drawing on extensive observations of children's play, he argues that well-designed structures allow even young children to experience small dangers and learn how to deal with these.

Window on research

Senda (1992) identifies a common sequence of behaviours in children's use of play structures. At a first stage of functional play, children use the equipment as intended, for example climbing up the steps and sitting to slide down. After some experience, children move on to a stage of technical play. Now enjoyment comes from exploring new ways of using the structure and from mastering new physical skills. It seems that the children in James' centre are seeking novel and challenging experiences in just this way. Finally, at a third stage of social play, children begin to use play structures as settings for group play, for example games of tag or pretend play.

Stephenson's (2003) research in early-years settings in New Zealand also highlights the importance for young children of physically challenging experiences: experiences that 4-year-olds in this study excitedly identify as 'scarey'. She argues for a need to balance the positive features of risk-taking for young children with narrower discourses of risk in the wider society. It seems that most children will seek novel and physically chal-lenging experiences on play structures, and this inevitably poses some risks. Therefore, practitioners need to acknowledge this as an issue and discuss their response as a team.

As one response, the provision of a safety surface under play structures is becoming increasingly common in early-years settings, as in public playgrounds. The aim is to increase opportunities for physical challenge, while providing protection from injuries. Norton et al. (2004) suggest that this is a complex area, and there is some debate about the effectiveness of different surfaces. They concluded that safety surfacing does seem to prevent overall injuries to children. However, fractures of the arm still occur when children fall from a height onto existing safety surfaces. This suggests that safety surfaces can provide only a partial response to the issue of risk. Good levels of staffing are also important to provide appropriate levels of supervision for more challenging play.

Because permanent play structures can become unchallenging after repeated use, some practitioners reject them. It is also undesirable to have a large structure that dominates the outdoor area, limiting other play options. Stephenson (2003), working with nursery children, highlights the value of movable equipment, for example tyres, crates, blocks, steps and planks. Provision of this kind allows children to participate in physically challenging experiences as they move equipment and design new structures. The environments created will be more diverse and offer greater novelty than most fixed structures. A-frames and ladders can be included to add variety and challenge.

Window on research

As a landscape architect, Herrington (2006) argues that challenge, including opportunities for physical challenge, represents one of the 'Seven Cs', the seven key criteria for successful outdoor spaces in childcare centres. However, observing children in Vancouver childcare settings, she identified a number of problems relating to the use of large play structures and their effect on other kinds of play. She also noted that simple design elements, including movable equipment, could provide valuable opportunities for challenge. For example, in one setting practitioners provided a simple tunnel that offered opportunities for children to crawl through the tunnel, balance on the tunnel and, later on, move the tunnel.

However, if movable equipment replaces large-scale fixed structures, some valuable opportunities for physical challenge, for example swinging and climbing to a height, may be lost. The issues here remain complex. Each setting will need to find its own solution, achieving its own balance between safety and challenge in the physical play curriculum.

This section has explored some of the recurring and complex issues that arise for practitioners who strive to develop outdoor play as a key vehicle for young children's learning. Most teams will need to allocate time for observation and subsequent discussion to resolve such issues. Decisions made will have implications for planning. There may be a need to adjust the long-term plans for a particular aspect of provision outdoors. Alternatively, changes may be required in daily planning that inform practitioners' interactions with children during specific activities. The next chapter considers curriculum planning as a tool to support practitioners in promoting children's development and learning through outdoor play.

Further Reading

Dickins, M. (2008) *Listening to Young Disabled Children*. London: National Children's Bureau.

McNaughton, G. (2000), *Rethinking Gender in Early Childhood Education*. London: Paul Chapman.

McNaughton, G. and Williams, G. (2009), *Teaching Young Children: Choices in Theory and Practice*, 2nd edn. Maidenhead, Berkshire: Open University.

Planning an outdoor curriculum in the early years

The most effective (excellent) settings (for enhancing child development) . . . achieve a balance between the opportunities provided for children to benefit from teacher-initiated group work and in the provision of freely chosen, yet potentially instructive, play activities. (Siraj-Blatchford and Sylva 2004, p. 720)

Outdoor environments offer rich opportunities for child- and adult-initiated play and activities that can support young children's development.

Window on research

Siraj-Blatchford and Sylva (2004) examined practice in a range of settings for 3- to 5-year-olds and their findings highlight the complexity of planning a curriculum to offer the right balance of experiences for this age group. While children seem to benefit from both freely chosen play activities and planned activities, the adult planned activities do need to be well matched to children's interests and development. It is important to note that child-initiated play includes instances where children play alone or with peers, and instances where adults join the play, supporting development and learning through interaction. Adults are more likely to interact with children in child-initiated play and activities in excellent settings rather than good settings. In excellent settings adults regularly support children's involvement in episodes of 'sustained shared thinking' (Siraj-Blatchford and Sylva 2004, p. 724). There is no simple prescription as to the ideal balance in terms of adult- and child-initiated play, and the ideal may well change for particular children over time.

It seems likely that a balance of experience is also appropriate for younger children, although the emphasis on freely chosen play is likely to be greater. Manning-Morton and Thorp (2003, p. 116) suggest that practitioners need to be sensitive to younger babies, working to achieve the right balance between 'scaffolding children's play with allowing their autonomous exploration and expression'.

These findings present a challenge for early-years curriculum planning across age groups, both indoors and outdoors. Through their planning, practitioners have to provide for an appropriate balance of adult- and child-initiated play and activities, they have to tune in to the interests of individual children and groups, they have to ensure that adults have opportunities to engage in sustained inter-actions with individual children and small groups, and they have to facilitate positive interactions between children. A further challenge outdoors is to plan to take advantage of the special affordances of outdoor spaces.

To meet these challenges, it is helpful to note the findings of researchers who have examined planning for this age group.

Window on research

Maynard and Waters (2007) studied outdoor play in four classes for 4–5-year-olds in Wales. The teachers of these classes had an idealized view of outdoor play in terms of its potential for enjoyment, self-direction and physical activity. However, to a considerable extent their approach to planning the outdoor curriculum mirrored their planning for indoors. These teachers only provided outdoor play and activities in good weather and they used 'predominantly teacher-directed tasks which focused on the learning of subject knowledge and basic skills' (Maynard and Waters 2007, p. 262). With the exception of some 'special activities' observed in two of the four schools, the teachers made limited use of natural environments where these were available. In addition, there was little evidence of planning for the potential of play and child-initiated activity as starting points for 'sustained shared thinking'. Maynard and Waters suggest several reasons for the divergence between the ideal-ized view of outdoor play and actual practice outdoors. In conclusion, they suggest that this duality in the teacher's thinking may relate to the tensions inherent in official curriculum guidance. Teachers who work within a curriculum framework that requires them to plan towards specified learning outcomes, while supporting learning that is child- and process-led, have a particular challenge to face in planning.

Further issues for planning an outdoor curriculum arise from Wood's (2007) discussion of play in early-years settings. Wood confirms the point above, suggesting that, even where practitioners value play, they may not understand how best to plan for play or understand their own role in supporting play-based learning. She also highlights the equity and social justice issues that arise in relation to a play-based curriculum, where children make choices that can cut across the needs and interests of other children. Wood (2007) identifies a further issue, one relating to play and cultural diversity. Free play and the notion of choice may be culturally unfamiliar to some young children. For example, some children in Brooker's (2005) study of young children's transition into a reception class came from Bangladeshi homes where they had been prepared to expect a formal and didactic approach to education. These children struggled to make sense of very different reception class expectations. One child's 'choice' was to resist adult attempts to engage her in play-based activity. As a result, some children from Bangladeshi homes appeared less competent than they in fact were. This suggests a need for teachers, during planning for outdoor play, to be alert to issues of choice.

Curriculum frameworks internationally

The starting point for planning is thinking about the purposes, goals or objectives of early-years education and care. These are likely to be shaped by different cultures, and so vary in important ways internationally (Spodek and Saracho 1996). For example, in 2000 Finland established a core curriculum for pre-school children for the year prior to school entry at age 7. One of the key objectives of this curriculum with relevance for outdoor play is 'to promote children's interest in nature and an idea of their own independence and responsibility for both nature and the man-made environment' (Ojala 2005). In England, in contrast, Early Years Foundation Stage (EYFS) practice guidance (DCSF 2008) relating to children up to 5 years places a high value on outdoor play, but this is framed within a set of early learning goals with a less explicit orientation towards environmental responsibility. 5-year-olds in England are expected to identify features of the natural world and express their views about this world, but not to take on responsibilities for this world. Te Whāriki (Ministry of Education 1996) provides a further contrast. Young children in New Zealand are expected to take responsibility for their environment in very practical ways, for example 'to develop skills in caring for the environment, such as cleaning, fixing, gardening, and helping others with self-care skills' (Ministry of Education 1996, p. 58). In the guidance on suitable experiences for toddlers, the suggestion is that children in this age group have opportunities to participate in purposeful activities, for example sweeping paths and using water to wash walls.

These are differences in terms of curriculum goals for children's engagement with the environment. However, there are more general dimensions of difference across countries that influence the purposes, goals or objectives of outdoor play and activity. One key dimension of difference can be seen in the emphasis that particular frameworks give to cognitive and affective learning, although these aspects of learning are likely to be interrelated (Eisner 1996). Curriculum planning has to balance these aspects, for example balancing a goal for 3-year-olds to count the stepping-stones with a goal for them to play co-operatively with peers. The nature of this balance is an area for debate, with different emphases across curricula. A further dimension of difference can be seen in the emphasis that frameworks give to curriculum content and the process of learning, and this has further implications for the planning of outdoor play.

This chapter examines how these dimensions of difference are reflected in particular curriculum frameworks, comparing frameworks from Flanders and the Netherlands, New Zealand and England. It begins by looking at the Experiential Education project, which Laevers (2000) initially developed as a new approach to pre-school education in Flanders and the Netherlands. Experiential Education places a high emphasis on the affective dimensions of learning and the process of learning. Young children's 'emotional well-being' and 'involvement' are two key concepts. It foregrounds the following aspects of learning in early childhood:

- emotional health;
- curiosity and the exploratory drive;
- expression and communication skills;
- imagination and creativity;
- the competence of self-organization;
- understanding the world of objects and people.

Experiential Education has influenced curricula and pedagogy in a number of countries internationally. In England, the influence can be seen in the work of the Effective Early Learning (EEL) project (Pascal and Bertram 1997), a distinctive approach to self-evaluation and action planning for early-years settings.

Te Whāriki (Ministry of Education 1996), the curriculum guidance for New Zealand, also prioritizes affective learning but with a focus on the principles of:

- empowerment;
- holistic development;
- family and community;
- relationships.

There is a similar emphasis on affective learning in the curriculum strands that flow from and interweave these principles:

- Well-being – *mana atua* (the health and well-being of the child are protected and nurtured).
- Belonging – *mana whenua* (children and their families feel a sense of belonging).
- Contribution – *mana reo* (opportunities for learning are equitable, and each child's contribution is valued).
- Exploration – *mana aoturoa* (the child learns through active exploration of the environment).

Te Whāriki identifies specific goals for learning and development within each of these strands, identified as knowledge, skills and attitudes. In addition, it links to essential skills and learning areas from the curriculum framework for schools. However, learning outcomes are described as indicative rather than definitive and there is an opportunity for those in each setting to establish their own curriculum priorities in relation to this framework. Planning for outdoor play, practitioners can choose to prioritize the development of peer relationships above the development of counting skills, if this seems most appropriate for a particular child or group.

In contrast, the EYFS practice guidance for English settings appears prescriptive, with early learning goals that 'establish expectations for most children to meet by the end of the reception year' (DCSF 2008). Early learning goals are conceptualized in terms of knowledge, skills, understanding and attitudes. They foreground children's cognitive learning, while also recognizing the importance of personal, social and emotional development. Early learning goals are organized within discrete areas of learning and development:

- Personal, social and emotional development.
- Communication, language and literacy.
- Problem-solving, reasoning and numeracy.
- Knowledge and understanding of the world.
- Physical development.
- Creative development.

The EYFS practice guidance does focus on the affective component of learning, with 'dispositions and attitudes' identified as a key aspect of personal, social and emotional development (DCSF 2008, p. 24). It also places the areas of learning and development in the context of a set of principles, grouped into four key themes, and these relate to a wider set of 16 commitments. The themes are:

- A unique child.
- Positive relationships.
- Enabling environments.
- Learning and development.

Every Child Matters (ECM) (DfES 2004) is a further framework, representing the wider policy agenda for children and young people's services in England. It proposes a broad set of outcomes, which are for children and young people to:

- be healthy;
- stay safe;
- enjoy and achieve;
- make a positive contribution;
- achieve economic well-being.

The *ECM* agenda represents a holistic approach to improving children's lives. It proposes that a range of children's services, including early-years services, works collaboratively to promote the five outcomes. Supporting this approach, the EYFS commitments (DCSF 2008) link to specific outcomes. For example, the commitment to 'respecting each other', within the theme of 'positive relationships', links to the *ECM* outcome for children to 'make a positive contribution'. However, while there is a clear focus on emotional well-being within these frameworks, the balance towards cognitive goals is greater than in some early-years curricula internationally, and this emphasis remains prescriptive. Returning to the previous example, an English practitioner would have to focus on both counting skills and peer relationships when planning for outdoor play.

Comparing these three frameworks, there is a significant overlap of purposes, goals and objectives. For example, a focus on the affective dimension of learning is common to all three frameworks, although differently identified as 'emotional health', 'well-being', and 'health and well-being'. All three frameworks take children's explorations as a key theme and all include a focus on relationships, although this is expressed as 'understanding the world of objects and people' in Experiential Education. Practitioners working in different countries, using any of the three frameworks, could plan to promote these aspects of development through outdoor play. However, the differences between frameworks are significant, and there are different challenges for practitioners working within each framework.

As noted by Maynard (2007), the challenge for the English approach to planning for outdoor play is to maintain a focus on the process of learning, while planning towards specific early learning goals. This is not an issue when planning for 'exploration and investigation', as an aspect of 'knowledge and understanding of the world'. Planning for 2-year-olds might focus on the process of exploring changes in dry sand when mixed with water poured from watering-cans. However, there could be a tension when planning for more content-based outcomes outdoors, for example 'recognize numerals 1 to 9'.

It is important to note that, even where a framework highlights learning goals within particular areas of learning, as in the English guidance (DCSF 2008), early learning is likely to flow over such boundaries. Many of the outdoor experiences most enjoyed by young children are rich in potential for cross-curricular learning. For example, 3-year-olds digging up potatoes in the garden are likely to be developing:

- large motor skills for digging the heavy soil;
- the scientific skills of observing and comparing potatoes of different shapes and sizes;
- mathematical language relating to shape and size;
- scientific knowledge and understanding of living things;
- communication and language skills for talking with peers and adults;
- self-control in waiting for a turn with a spade.

Extending the practical activity, a practitioner could introduce a picture book about vegetables to share, supporting early literacy skills, while children could represent and communicate experiences

---

REFLECTION POINT

What is the potential for cross-curricular learning for toddlers playing outdoors after a heavy fall of snow?

Using the Early Years Foundation Stage areas of learning from English guidance, what is the potential to support children's:

- personal, social and emotional development;

- communication, language and literacy;

- problem-solving, reasoning and numeracy;

- knowledge and understanding of the world;

- physical development;

- creative development?

in the garden through the additional languages of collage, drawing and painting. With skilled and sensitive teaching, all aspects of this experience could help shape children's positive dispositions towards learning.

Each setting will need to make decisions about the approach to planning, informed by a range of factors. These will include national or more local curriculum frameworks and guidance, distinctive features of the setting, including the practitioners' shared philosophy, and finally the team's reflections on their own experience of working with children outdoors. Planning as a team is valuable. It promotes professional development, providing a context within which practitioners can share and analyse their observations of children, and ideas to support future learning. The conflicts that arise within teams, if sensitively handled, can initiate deeper levels of thinking about individual children and the outdoor curriculum.

Whatever approach to planning that practitioners use, they will want to ensure that written plans do not limit the opportunities for learning that arise spontaneously. Therefore, it will be important to use planning in flexible ways. This is particularly important outdoors, where unpredictability is a feature of the environment. Daily planning, for example, can never predict children's sudden excitement at the appearance of a rainbow or a noisy police helicopter overhead. Unpredictable events are often the most exciting and engaging events for children as well as many adults.

The observation and planning cycle

Despite the unpredictability of outdoor experience, the quality of children's learning outdoors is likely to relate to the quality of planning, whatever form this takes. However, as Perry's (2001) study of outdoor role-play in an American kindergarten suggests, effective planning is not an isolated activity. To promote the development and learning of individuals as well as groups of children, planning can be seen as part of a continuous cycle, closely linked to the observation, recording and analysis of children's learning. In some early-years traditions, the focus is primarily on the learning and development of individual children, an approach encouraged by the English and Welsh frameworks. In other traditions, such as the pre-schools of Reggio Emilia, planning supports a process of group learning, where several children are involved in the shared development of thinking.

To meet the challenge of planning for children's learning and development through both child-led free play and adult-led group activities outdoors, it is helpful to consider planning at three different levels: long term, medium term and short term. The section below looks at the purposes and key features of these different kinds of planning. It uses both real-life and fictional case studies to exemplify key ideas and issues. The real-life case studies come from the well-documented research and development work of Susan Herrington, a landscape designer. The section begins by looking at two different aspects of long-term planning for outdoor play: first, the design of outdoor spaces; and second, the long-term plans for areas of provision outdoors.

Long-term planning: designing the outdoor space

The long-term planning of environments for outdoor play and learning is about planning the structure and the elements of environments that will be relatively stable over time, and that provide for continuity in children's experiences. A well-designed outdoor space should offer rich opportunities for learning and development, supporting both child-led free play and, where appropriate, adult-initiated group activities.

The structures and the elements of the play environment can include hard landscaping such as paths, low walls, pergolas and boulders. They can also include soft landscaping such as trees, bushes, sand and soil. The range and quality of these structures and elements shape the opportunities for learning. Herrington (2005) notes a tendency to think of the outdoor space of an early-years setting as if it was an empty floor space. Practitioners fill their empty space with equipment and resources taken from a storage shed or an indoor classroom and return these at the end of the session. An empty outdoor space has few stable structures and elements, except perhaps a perimeter fence, a tarmac yard and a closely mown patch of grass. Without the equipment and resources from the shed, it is likely to be a boring space for children and adults, offering limited opportunities for learning and development.

However, if we consider our most intense memories of play as children, equipment and toys probably played a minor part. On a beach, in the woods, or on pockets of neglected, urban wasteland, it is the spaces and materials of the landscape that invite children to play and that shape their experiences. Therefore, long-term planning for outdoor spaces should include the design of structures and elements that offer diverse spaces for play, as well as diverse materials and plants to support play through the changing seasons and in different kinds of weather.

Case study: planning an infant garden

Having identified limitations in the 'empty floor space' approach to outdoor play, Herrington (2005) exemplifies an alternative approach through her account of the design of her Infant Garden. As a landscape designer, Herrington carried out an experiment, redesigning the featureless outdoor space for the youngest children at a day-care setting. She wanted to see how the long-term features of a natural landscape might support young children's learning, describing the new garden as an 'outdoor play landscape that would support the sensorimotor and socio-emotional development of infants as it occurred in spontaneous exploration' (Herrington 2005, p. 219).

In the redesigned garden, the simple elements of soil, plants, sand and stones provided a rich resource for children's exploratory play. Key features of the design were a large circular sand tray shaded by a parachute canopy, a maze with five different edible plants, a trail of stepping-stones out into the garden, a circle of pine trees and a variety of plants. Herrington (2005) and her students, who had watched children at play in the original yard, observed the children at play in their new garden and compared these observations. The comparison showed an increase in young children's spatial explorations and in the range, complexity and/or intensity of a number of play behaviours. Herrington's observations suggested the rich potential of natural landscapes to support young children's social, emotional, physical and cognitive development. This experiment helps to make the case for investing time and resources in the design and development of natural play landscapes for young children. There is value in reviewing approaches based on filling empty spaces with manufactured toys and structures.

Defining spaces

One of the successful features of Herrington's design in the case study above is her use of hard and soft landscaping to define spaces, creating distinctive spaces for different kinds of play.

Window on research

Doctoroff 's (2001) review of research findings for indoor spaces confirms the value of defining spaces. The review suggests that complex play and increased levels of interaction between peers can be achieved by defining spaces with visible boundaries. This is sometimes called zoning when talking about outdoor spaces.

Bilton (2002) also suggests that zoning can impact positively on the way in which children use and care for resources (Bilton 2002). As with Herrington's (2005) garden, fixed and aesthetically pleasing divisions of space can be used outdoors, for example walls, seats, trellis and plantings. Where space is limited and needs to be used more flexibly, changeable divisions can be improvised, for example planted tubs, resource trolleys, crates and tyres. However, although defining spaces is an important strategy in the design of play environments, it is important to allow flexible use of materials within this design.

Case study: stepping-stones

Herrington (2005) designed a modification of a school playground for 2–6-year-olds. A simple, winding pathway of 20 stepping-stones was introduced, taking children from the doorway of the school into the yard, to the play equipment and then on to a part of the yard that was rarely played in before. Observations of the children's play showed that this pathway helped to extend children's exploration of the environment. It was a relatively small-scale change but it modified the children's use of space in significant ways.

Window on research

Herrington (2006), in her study of the design of outdoor spaces in a sample of childcare centres in Vancouver, noted that children were less likely to engage in sustained play in centres where the use of these resources was tightly controlled. Children played for longer when they were free to transport and mix these materials. In addition, staff spent less time controlling children's play. This would allow more time for staff to engage in sustained interactions with individuals and small groups.

Pathways are another important design element within outdoor play spaces. They can be made from a variety of materials, including bricks, paving stones and gravel. The simplest form of pathway is a worn grass path. Pathways that lead to a particular place or to somewhere hidden are the most enticing. A garden for 2- and 3-year-olds had a worn grass path overhung with trees that led to a willow tepee, offering an invitation to adventure.

Plants

Plantings can make an important contribution to the design of outdoor areas. Trees in particular can transform an empty and uninteresting space in just a few years. Native trees are a relatively inexpensive resource if bought when small. Therefore, in most gardens it should be possible to include a small wild area at the edge of the garden that is attractive to wildlife. As well as native trees, shrubs and flowers, in many gardens this area can include a bird feeding station, a log pile and small pieces of carpet on the grass, providing a dark hiding place for minibeasts.

Case study: a wild area

Herrington (2005) describes a project that involved making subtle changes to a kindergarten play yard in the United States. A small area of grass in the corner of the yard was allowed to grow. This had been an uninteresting and a static place previously. However, this small area soon became a special place. The children imagined how high the grass might grow, they made patterns by flattening the grass, they played hide and seek, and they enjoyed searching out the flowers and minibeasts that began to appear. The little patch of grass was so special that when the maintenance workers arrived to mow it down, the children blocked the way. Their views of what was important in the garden were made very clear and the maintenance workers were sent away until the end of the school year.

Long-term planning: areas of provision

Long-term plans can be developed for specific areas of play provision. Linked to indoor plans, these highlight the ways in which outdoor provision complements and extends indoor learning. For example, long-term plans for an indoor water tray could be linked to outdoor planning that allows children to explore the properties of water on a more expansive scale and with fewer restrictions on the messy elements of play. Rather than simply duplicating indoor provision, it is important to think through the distinctive opportunities for learning outdoors.

REFLECTION POINT

Think about how to provide for exploratory outdoor water play for toddlers or young children on a large scale.

Imagine you have £50 to spend in a large DIY store.

- What resources would you buy?
- How would you set these up?
- How would you support the play as an adult?
- What are the safety issues to consider?

Continuous or near-continuous provision outdoors can support the learning of children at very different stages of development and with different approaches to learning. This is a useful approach to use from the point when children are confidently mobile outdoors.

Illustration 5.1: Water play

Open-ended resources such as sand and water can be used in different ways by children who are at different levels in terms of knowledge, understanding and skills. The opportunities that are offered for children to repeat experiences are important and enable children to consolidate their learning (Rushton and Larkin 2001). In particular, the predictability of continuous provision enables children to plan their learning and to develop and extend ideas over time.

A large play area for older children would be able to incorporate all or most of the areas of provision suggested below, with a wide choice of resources. A smaller play area for children between 1 and 2 years could incorporate several areas, depending on the interest of the group. It would be appropriate to keep the range of resources relatively restricted so as not to overwhelm children with too many choices.

Key areas of outdoor provision to include are:

An area or areas for natural materials
This can include wet and dry sand, water and soil. Additional materials can be provided at times, for example bark chippings, autumn leaves or shingle in a giant tractor tyre. A range of resources can be provided to support the exploration of these materials, including containers of various sizes, spades and shovels, pipes and guttering. It is also valuable to provide equipment for transporting materials such as trucks and wheelbarrows.

Illustration 5.2: Sand tray

A large construction area
This can include hollow blocks, crates, tyres and planks. Props to support imaginative play can be provided, for example a steering wheel, blankets, dolls and mark-making materials in a carry-box.

A den area
A den building area might be an extension of the large construction area. It can include cardboard boxes, a clothes horse, a variety of fabric and large pegs.

A quiet area
Set out on a rug or table, this area could include small construction materials, jigsaws, mathematical apparatus such as small building blocks or a dolls' house. It would be appropriate to change resources in relation to children's changing interests.

A creative area
This can incorporate painting in various forms, including painting on easels, and tables. Large-scale painting can be done on large sheets of paper on the floor or attached to fencing. Mark-making materials can be included, including chunky chalks for the floor or wall. A portable box with paper, card, notebooks, pencils and adhesive tape is a valuable resource that children can take to different parts of the play area.

A music area
A small selection of percussion instruments on a rug or low table can be included in this area. Nursery-rhyme books and a collection of scarves to use for dancing are a useful addition.

Small apparatus
Appropriate apparatus would be a basketball net and ball, bats and balls, quoits, beanbags and hoops.

Physical activity space
If space is available, a large space for running and physical games, including ball games and tag, should be provided.

A physical play area
Climbing equipment can be provided on a safety surface. Loose pieces that can be assembled in different ways offer flexibility and variety, for example tunnels, hidey cubes, steps, planks, A-frames and ladders.

A role-play area
One or more role-play areas can be included:

- A garage and/or car wash role-play area can extend play with wheeled toys. This can include a petrol pump, a cash register, tool set, car manuals, a Highway Code, an AA book and laminated maps.

- Home-corner resources can provide a link between indoor and outdoor play, for example a hob and kitchen equipment, tea set, dolls, soft toys and pushchairs. A bucket of water can be used to extend play with the tea set.
- A baby bathing area can be created with a baby bath on crates or a table, dolls to bathe, towels and a baby-changing area.
- A shop structure can be used to develop shopping play, with shopping baskets, wallets, purses and bags.

A roadway area
A permanent or improvised roadway area can be developed with props, including traffic signs, road markings and numbered parking bays. This might link to the garage role play outlined above. Dressing-up resources can be included, for example helmets and tabards for firefighters.

A garden area
A garden area can be developed for growing flowers and vegetables. Plants can be grown in borders, in a chequerboard garden, raised beds, hanging baskets, tubs and painted tyres. Watering-cans with a bucket of water can be provided.

Number area
A number area could include small apparatus games such as coloured bean-bags to be thrown into coloured buckets. It could also include a number washing-line, number cards for hop-scotch, skittles and a giant dice for number games. The area could link to a book corner, with a selection of number stories, songs and rhymes that can be acted out.

A book corner
An outdoor book corner could include rugs, blankets, chairs, a large log or crates as seating. There should be different kinds of books, including books that relate to outdoor interests. It could also incorporate a laminated weather chart, with books about the weather, as well as laminated song and rhyme sheets.

Areas of provision can be provided on different scales, depending on budget and available space. For example, a crate with three small percussion instruments could serve as a music area. Alternatively,

Illustration 5.3: Numbers

giant-sized percussion instruments or musical mobiles could be provided as a permanent feature.

It is important to ensure a balance of activities, with space for vigorous, active play, as well as space for quieter play. Some children, particularly children who are new to the setting, may need tempting out into outdoor areas and are likely to be frightened or overwhelmed by an area that is dominated by active play.

While most outdoor provision works well as discrete areas, flexibility is important. It may be appropriate for some play to flow between areas. For example, in large play areas, play with bikes, scooters and trolleys is enhanced when children have opportunities to make real journeys between interesting places. A wide and winding track for wheeled toys could pass through, for example, a role-play area, large construction area and wild area. Each stop offers

---

OBSERVATION POINT

Undertake some observations in a well-developed and varied outdoor play area.

- What spaces do children use for quieter play in pairs or groups of three?

- What is the quality of peer interaction?

- What is special about the places that children choose?

---

opportunities for social or imaginative interaction. In smaller areas, bike play that spills out into other kinds of play can be intrusive and sometimes dangerous. A more confined and flexible roadway area may be appropriate. Adults can involve children in discussion of roadway design and the need to avoid interrupting other activities by drawing the roadway during the session with playground chalk.

The case study that follows provides an example of a team working on long-term planning for an area of provision for 3–5-year-olds.

Case study: planning a large construction area

Narinder had recently joined Cross Flatts Nursery School and had special responsibility for mathematical and technological learning. After a term, Narinder shared her observations with the team and discussed development work in the outdoor area. As a newcomer, she had observed that mathematical learning was a strength of the setting but was mainly focused indoors. In terms of technology, children worked well with small construction sets, but other activities seemed to be too adult-directed, offering few opportunities for children to develop their own ideas. The large and attractive outdoor space could be important in providing a large construction area to strengthen these two aspects of the curriculum.

The team worked over a number of months, developing plans. As they discussed resources, Miriam also shared ideas developed from her reading. She wanted the team to provide open-ended resources, for example blocks, crates, tyres and planks, allowing children to create their own role-play environments. A wheeled trolley would be particularly useful, functioning as bus, lorry, ambulance or fire engine, depending on the children's chosen play theme. Miriam explained how social interaction and language use improves when children use open-ended materials and have to negotiate meanings. The team were encouraged that Miriam's and Narinder's ideas seemed to mesh so well.

Illustration 5.4 shows the team's long-term planning for the large construction area. It uses the framework of the English practice guidance (DCSF 2008) but incorporates aspects of thinking about learning dispositions from Te Whāriki (Ministry of Education 1996).

WHAT WILL THE CHILDREN LEARN?

Skills:

Designing and constructing
Planning
Predicting
Identifying problems/problem-solving
Evaluating
Comparing
Marching and sorting
Counting
Sharing and co-operating
Communicating
Negotiating
Asking questions
Imagining
Taking on a role
Climbing, jumping, balancing
Reading and mark-making

Learning dispositions:

Taking an interest
Being involved
Persisting with challenge and difficulty
Expressing an idea / feeling / point of view
Taking responsibility

Knowledge and understanding of:

Materials, e.g. wood, plastic, rubber, net
Balance and symmetry
Shape and space
Measurement
Size
Transportation
Position, e.g. on, off, under, behind
Connection
Horizontality and verticality
Grids
Enclosure and envelopment
Adult roles
Print

KEY EARLY LEARNING GOALS

Knowledge and understanding of the world:

• Ask questions about why things happen and how things work.
• Build and construct with a wide range of objects, selecting appropriate resources, and adapting their work where necessary.
• Investigate objects and materials by using all of their senses as appropriate.

Physical development:

• Show awareness of space, of themselves and of others.
• Use a range of small and large equipment.

Problem-solving, reasoning and numeracy:

• Use developing mathematical ideas and methods to solve practical problems.
• Use language such as 'circle' or 'bigger' to describe the shape and size of solids and flat shapes.
• Use everyday words to describe position.

Creative development:
• Explore colour, texture, shape, form and space in two or three dimensions.

- Use their imagination in art and design – and role play.
- Express and communicate their ideas, thoughts and feelings by using a widening range of materials, suitable tools, imaginative and role play, movement, designing and making . . .

RESOURCES

Hollow blocks
Crates, tyres, cones, ropes
Trolley
Toolset, measuring tape
Mark-making box
Book box with fiction and non-fiction books
Laminated song and rhyme sheets
Album of photos of children's work
Box of fabric
Pegs

THE ADULT ROLE

Make continuous provision with regular adult observation and interaction.
Encourage children to experiment with the materials.
Introduce appropriate vocabulary and questions to extend children's thinking.
Take on a play-tutoring role with inexperienced children.
Provide supplementary resources in labelled baskets.
Take digital photographs of children working.
Introduce laminated sheets of photos and albums as a stimulus to ideas.
Introduce props in response to children's ideas and play themes.
Introduce 'girl day' sessions if the area is dominated by boys.

Illustration 5.4: Long-term planning for a large construction area

Evaluating long-term plans

It is important for teams to evaluate planning for outdoor learning. The evaluation of long-term plans is considered in detail here. It is important to give similar consideration to the evaluation of medium- and short-term plans.

Long-term plans for key areas of outdoor provision can be reviewed over time, perhaps focusing on an area every six to eight weeks. When monitoring an area, it is useful to ask general questions about how the area is working, for example:

- Which children work in the area?
- How regularly do children return to the area?
- What is the approximate length of time children stay in the area?
- What do children do and say in the area?
- What are children learning in the area?

An observation record (Illustration 5.5) on a clipboard can support practitioners in undertaking regular but brief observations.

As practitioners evaluate areas, they can draw on their observation to ask questions and make judgements about the effectiveness of the outdoor provision. For example, practitioners evaluating the outdoor construction area might ask:

- Do girls and boys regularly become involved in designing and building?
- Are children identifying problems and finding solutions to problems?
- Are children using mathematical language to talk about shape and space?

Judgements made can inform decisions about necessary changes to enhance the opportunities for learning outdoors. The observation record also provides ideas for supporting the learning of groups and individuals who are working at very different levels.

An additional approach to evaluation of the outdoor curriculum involves monitoring across areas of provision. Here, the focus of monitoring could be on the opportunities for learning within a

---

AREA OF PROVISION: LARGE CONSTRUCTION

Date: 20.01.09

Children	Activity, language and learning	Next steps
Amrit, Davinder Megan	Worked co-operatively, building. A princess castle. Enclosure made with crates. Cones placed on top. Amrit: 'Let's make our bed here cos it's bedtime now and the princesses are tired.' (1 hr approx.)	Introduce books about castles. Note architecture, e.g. turrets. Suggest drawing plans of castles.
Connor	Working alone, loads crates onto trolley and transports across playground. Tips crates in a pile. 'I've got loads of bricks.' (10 mins)	Encourage and support play with play partner. Look at photos of simple constructions.
Mohammed, Jack	Placed crates in a horizontal line. Added tyres vertically. 'We're friends, right.' 'Yeh, mate.'	Provide a commentary on actions, e.g.'That crate's going next to that one. You're making a line now.'

Illustration 5.5: An observation record

specific curriculum area, for example ICT. Alternatively, the focus could be on an aspect of the curriculum such as cultural diversity. The next case study provides an example of monitoring a curriculum area.

Case study: monitoring the use of ICT

The staff at Hillcrest Early Years Centre had recently attended in-service training focused on ICT. They were particularly interested in approaches used in British, Portuguese and Swedish settings (Siraj-Blatchford and Siraj-Blatchford 2003), where ICT had been integrated into aspects of play-based provision. All agreed on the value of increasing children's awareness of the uses of ICT in everyday contexts, to promote positive dispositions towards learning about and through ICT. It was decided that development work would start with an audit of provision indoors and outdoors, followed by a listing of possible developments (Illustration 5.6, opposite). Although aware that ICT might not link to all areas of provision, they decided to consider each area in turn.

Medium-term planning for outdoor learning

Areas of outdoor play provision, which are available continuously or near continuously, provide the main context for children's learning outdoors. However, there are times when medium-term themes or enhancements, planned in response to children's interests and thinking, can enrich opportunities for learning outdoors. These may arise from predictable and interesting events, for example a cold spell of wintry weather that promises frost, ice and possibly snow. They can also be developed from children's observed interests. Children's preoccupation with the schemas of going through and enveloping (Athey 2007), for example, can provide a useful starting point for building dens or a role-play camp. Favourite stories, such as *The Three Billy Goats Gruff*, also provide starting points for medium-term enhancements of provision.

Some medium-term plans will focus solely on outdoor provision, for example a focus on dens. However, in many cases medium-term planning will offer links between indoor and outdoor learning. For example, children's fascination with the first spring bulbs in the garden might be supported and extended through creative work using a variety of art media, both indoors and outdoors.

When planning themes and enhancements, the duration should be flexible and responsive to children's interests. However, it is important to note the importance of repetition for young children's learning. This is evidenced by children's repeated requests for favourite

OUTDOOR ICT AUDIT

Outdoor provision	Existing ICT provision	Possible ICT provision
Wet and dry sand		
Painting area		
Water area		
Digging areas		
Large construction		Mobile phones. Programmable toy vehicles.
Small construction		
Mark-making area		
Music area		Battery-operated children's tape-recorder for music.
Garden area		
Wild area		
Physical area		
Role-play area	Telephone box. Toy microwave.	Mobile phones. Electric till for shop. Walkie-talkies (police and fire-fighter role play).
Roadway	Traffic lights.	Mobile phones. Electronic till for garage. Calculator in garage. Programmable toy vehicles.
Book area		Album of outdoor photos taken with digital camera.
General provision		Digital camera.
Related indoor provision		Video clips and internet. Links extending outdoor experiences, e.g. butterfly life-cycle.

Illustration 5.6: Outdoor ICT audit

stories, songs and rhymes. Elliot (1999) suggests that repeated experiences are not only enjoyable but help to reinforce valuable neural pathways in the brain. To ensure that outdoor environments offer opportunities for repeated experience and allow children to consolidate and extend learning, it is important that key activities and experiences are offered over time. Children, for example, may enjoy the novelty of a role-play garage for a week, but they are likely to gain more from involvement in the development of a play theme over a more extended period.

Two case studies below consider medium-term planning. The first is for a class of 4- and 5-year-olds, and the second is for a small group of under-2s.

Case study: medium-term planning around favourite stories

Lian and Jim worked in the Karinga Infant School reception class. They had noticed that two favourite picture books were stories about young children playing outdoors. One of these, *Sally's Secret* (Hughes 1992) centred on a girl of about 4 who loved finding places in which to hide. She made houses in all sorts of secret places, both alone and with her best friend. Lian and Jim felt that this story, with its bird, ladybird and cat, each welcomed as visitors into the girl's secret house, captured the reception children's delight in being outdoors, close to the natural world. Another favourite story, *Whistle for Willie* (Keats 1964) was set in the contrasting urban landscape of an American city. In this story, Peter also enjoyed finding places in which to hide, and playing at grown-ups, in this case accompanied by his dog Willie.

Lian and Jim used the two books to stimulate talk about what the reception children liked most outdoors. Dens, animals and playing with friends were high on the list. This seemed to be a great starting point for a summertime enhancement of the reception garden. Thinking through their plans, Lian and Jim were particularly pleased to have an opportunity to develop a focus on friendship. Two new children had recently joined the class, and one of them, Carly, was having difficulty settling into the group. Lian and Jim felt that the planned activities would provide a good context for supporting integration of the new children.

Following discussions, Lian and Jim drew up a medium-term plan (Illustration 5.7, opposite), drawing on the Experiential Education curriculum framework (Laevers 2000).

KARINGA RECEPTION CLASS: MEDIUM-TERM PLANNING

Focus of interest / theme: Outdoor play stories, songs and rhymes

Date: June 2003   *Expected duration: 4 weeks*

Key learning goals:

- Emotional health.
- Curiosity and the exploratory drive.
- Expression and communication skills.
- Imagination and creativity.
- The competence of self-organization.
- Understanding the world of objects and people.

Focus activities and experiences:

- Listen to and discuss stories and rhymes about outdoor play.
- Talk about special friends and make sure that everyone has a play partner.
- Negotiate and record plans for dens and secret houses.
- Build and evaluate dens and secret houses using a variety of materials.
- Explore the properties of materials to keep out the sun on hot days and keep out the rain on wet days.
- Use language to create roles and stories while playing in dens and secret houses.
- Search for and closely observe animals in the garden, e.g. birds, spiders, ladybirds, beetles, worms, butterflies.
- Use books, video clips and the internet to find out more about the animals observed.
- Record observations of animals through drawing, painting, collage and clay work.

Resources:

- Wild area.
- Crates, blocks, logs.
- Folding clothes-dryer.
- Quadro frames.
- Variety of fabrics, e.g. net, cotton, muslin, plastic, wool.

- Variety of joining materials, e.g. pegs, bulldog clips, string, masking tape.
- Role-play props, e.g. tea-set, dolls, soft animals.
- Natural materials for role play, e.g. pine cones, pebbles, shells.
- Laminated song and rhyme sheets, e.g. 'Ladybird, ladybird, fly away home'.
- Outdoor stories, e.g. 'Sally's Secret', 'Whistle for Willie'
- Magnifiers.
- Reference books about birds and mini-beasts.
- Art boards for outdoor drawing, pencils, charcoal, pastels.
- Indoor art area, computers and video.

Appropriate questions (present, future, past):

- What materials will you need?
- How will you join the materials?
- How will you make it strong?
- Which material do you think will keep out the hot sun/wet rain?
- What do you think will happen if . . . ?
- Was it a good house? In what ways? How could you have made it better?
- What can you see if you look very closely? What is it doing?

Appropriate vocabulary:

- Large, small, shape, space, straight, tall, long, wide, high, narrow.
- Join, connect, fasten.
- Strong, weak.
- Warm, cool, wet, dry, waterproof, shade.
- Net, cotton, muslin, plastic, wool, card, foil, wood.
- Pine cones, pebbles, shells, soil, grass.
- Bird names, spider, ladybird, beetle, ant, worm, caterpillar, butterfly, centipede.
- Soft, smooth, slippery, furry, spiky, prickly, shiny.

Involvement of parents/carers:

- Send song and rhyme sheets home.
- Send home tally sheet for children to record animals seen at home in a day.
- Invite parent/family helpers to support the work.

Illustration 5.7: Medium-term planning

At the end of this successful focus, Lian and Jim evaluated their planning and the work undertaken, to inform future practice. They asked questions relating to the following aspects:

- Timing.
- Manageability.
- The balance of child-initiated and adult-directed work.
- Matching to children's interests.
- Matching to children's developmental levels.
- Quality and range of resources.
- Involvement of parents/carers.
- Evidence of children's learning.

Case study: medium-term planning for a building site focus

Jessie lived close to Oakwood Child-care Centre and she enjoyed walking to the centre with her son Jack in his pushchair before setting off for a job in the city. Jack was 18 months old and had been at the centre for two months now. Jessie was very pleased with how well he had settled, but was a bit worried at his apparent lack of sharing skills. He was a first child and so had little experience of sharing at home and she had seen him snatch toys from other children several times at nursery. In the last week, work had started on the large building site that Jessie and Jack passed on their way to the centre. They had watched as large bulldozers flattened the ground, and now a crane had been brought onto the site. Jack was so excited by this new event that he was very cross when Jessie insisted it was time to stop watching and go to the centre.

When they got to the centre, Jack was still cross, and Simon, his key person, asked what the matter was. Jessie and Jack between them managed to explain, and so Simon took Jack off to find his favourite book about diggers when Jessie had gone. His crossness soon disappeared as he became engrossed in looking at the different diggers and listening to the simple story. When it was time to go outside, Jack was still holding onto his book about diggers and was quite reluctant to join any other play.

Simon made some quick notes in Jack's profile about his interest in the building site and in the book about diggers. He also noted how Jack had sadly said, at the end of the story, 'digger gone'. This was one of the first times that staff had heard him put two words together. Simon took Jack's profile along to the planning meeting the next day, together with profiles for his other children. Discussing Jack's reluctance to give up his diggers book to any other children, Simon suggested an idea for an enhancement of the outdoor sand tray. This seemed to be the right time to introduce a building site theme into the sand play, resourcing the area with a variety of large diggers, some new books about building sites and some laminated song and rhyme sheets. The team agreed to develop a medium-term plan for this enhancement. It seemed to be an interest that was likely to last for several weeks and could possibly last until all the new homes on the site were completed.

Short-term planning for outdoor learning

Early-years settings are complex organizations and may include children with diverse needs. Usually, there is a wide range of activities on offer and there will be at least two adults in the staff team. A variety of other adults may be present, including parents, carers, students and other professionals. In complex settings of this kind, short-term planning is the key to ensuring that long- and medium-term plans for the outdoor area are effectively realized. Short-term planning provides a framework for focused teaching with individuals, as well as small and large groups. It can be used to ensure an appropriate balance in the adult support provided for adult-initiated and child-initiated play and activities. The case study below considers issues relating to short-term planning for outdoor play.

Case study: short-term planning

At the Bennett Street Nursery weekly staff meeting, Di and Woan Chan shared their recent observations of children's learning in the outdoor area. The children in the group were 3 to 4 years old and there were several children in the group who still flitted from activity to activity with few signs of involvement. Both practitioners were concerned that the current staff rota, moving adults between areas several times a day, was contributing to superficial levels of adult engagement with play. This seemed to be particularly problematic outdoors, where some staff took on a primarily supervisory role. Although children played happily outside, conflicts were relatively common, and more complex play unusual. Both practitioners felt frustrated by a lack of opportunity to tackle these problems in a sustained way, and proposed changes to the staffing schedule to allow staff to focus on each area for a week. They hoped that this would support higher levels of engagement by both children and staff. Some staff opposed the change, primarily because weather conditions sometimes made the outdoor role difficult. However, with agreement to allow for flexibility in poor weather, the team decided to trial this new approach. The new weekly planning grid, with indoor and outdoor focus activities, is shown in Illustration 5.8.

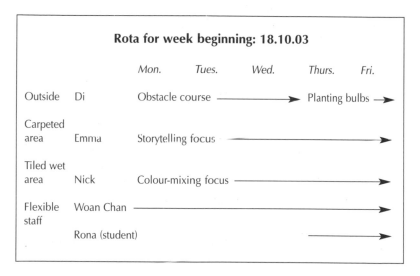

Illustration 5.8: Weekly rota and focus activities

The Bennett Street team agreed to retain other effective aspects of their short-term planning. Their observation focus worked well, and this, with evaluations of focus activities, was important in feeding back into future planning. They also liked having three adults responsible for areas, while the fourth and any additional adults were used more flexibly. This flexibility was particularly important when large numbers of children chose to play outside. It also meant that an adult was available to provide support when someone was leading an activity such as planting bulbs. The team was particularly keen to retain a balance of adult time between focus activities, developed from long- and medium-term plans, and engagement with the spontaneous child-led events of the day.

The Bennett Street team had agreed to focus regularly on physical play. They wanted all children to enjoy active, physical play, and they aimed to provide appropriate levels of challenge for physically confident children. This week's outdoor planning for an obstacle course was drawn from long-term plans for the physical area (Illustration 5.9, opposite). The second outdoor plan was for a focus on planting bulbs, drawn from long-term plans for the garden area.

At the end of the week, however, the weather changed from warm and sunny to persistent rain. The ground was muddy and it was not good weather for planting bulbs. However, the team had in place some flexible planning for a rainy day, supported by a range of resources stored in boxes. These included spare wellies and waterproof clothes, a variety of umbrellas, containers, pipes and guttering for collecting, measuring and moving water, as well as several story books and laminated cards with songs and rhymes about rainy weather. Despite some short bursts of heavy rain, Di was able to work effectively outdoors through the week, with groups of children enthusiastic to play out in the rain or to watch with fascination from the shelter of a small play-house.

The adult role

Consideration of the adult role is a key aspect of planning for outdoor play and an important consideration at each level of planning. The adult role as educator is far more concerned with interaction than the primarily supervisory role of adults during school playtimes or lunch periods.

Window on research

Perry's (2001) case study of an American nursery school suggests that, although skilled practitioners will often leave children to play independently, this should arise from a careful judgement about how, when or if to intervene, based on detailed observations of individuals and groups.

Research suggests a key role for adults in supporting young children's learning, particularly through language (Wood et al. 1980; Wells 1987; Nind 2001; Siraj-Blatchford et al. 2002).

BENNETT STREET NURSERY: SHORT-TERM PLANNING

Adult: Di

Focus area: Physical development
Activity area/s: Outdoor physical area

Learning goals:
To explore movement to travel around, under, over and through large apparatus.
To use language to talk about actions.

Monitoring and assessment:
Observe children's levels of confidence, motivation to explore movement and use of language to talk about actions.

Grouping:
Friendship groups of up to four.

Individual needs:
Extension: explore and describe new ways of moving.
New children learning English as an Additional Language: focus on highlighted vocabulary.
Encourage participation with adult support: Maria, Sian, Kiranjit, Jamie.

Activity:
Children help to set up the obstacle course, explaining how the apparatus could be used.
Free movement on the obstacle course.

Resources:
Hollow blocks and planks, hurdles, flexible and rigid tunnels, plastic steps, hoops, rope.

Key questions:
Questions about the present: e.g. What are you doing? Which part is touching the bench?
Questions about the future: e.g. How could you do it differently next time?
Questions about the past: e.g. Can you remember how you first moved through the tunnel . . . and then how you did it?

Key vocabulary:
Provide a commentary on actions, e.g. 'You are high up.'
Names of apparatus, body parts, high, low, around, under, over, through, on, top, slow, fast, slide, pull, crawl, wriggle, stretch, jump.

Illustration 5.9: Short-term planning

Nind (2001), who led an action-research study focused on language development in the early-years unit of a London primary school, identified a special role for outdoor play as an effective context for children's talk. These studies suggest the need for adults to adopt an informal, conversational style outdoors, following the lead of children's play and talk. It seems that more controlling and managerial adult styles place unintended blocks on opportunities for learning through language. Siraj-Blatchford et al. (2002, p. 10) suggest that the most effective adult–child interactions take place over longer periods than more typically brief adult–child exchanges and incorporate elements of 'sustained shared thinking'.

Adults have a key role as conversational partners during outdoor play. The role of play tutor (Aubrey et al. 2000), where the adult joins in play to provide a model and to suggest or extend play ideas, is also an important one. This is particularly important where adults are working with children who are inexperienced players.

The final case study provides a real-life example of an adult in this modelling role as she implements her short-term planning. The story and photographs are from Parklands Children's Centre.

Case study: We're going on a bear hunt

Gina and Helen were outdoors and, although the weather was cold with light rain, a large group of children had chosen to play outdoors. Helen was playing at the sand tray with a new child, Imran, and Gina was leading on the week's focus activity for outdoors. This involved supporting the 3- and 4-year-olds in reading and acting out the *We're Going on a Bear Hunt* story, using the version by Michael Rosen and Helen Oxenbury (1993). The team had chosen this story as the focus of short-term planning because several team members had noticed the children's love of scary stories and rhymes. Books with grizzly bears and monsters were a real favourite at storytimes and several of the children loved to act out these stories, both within the confines of the indoor setting at storytimes as well as outdoors.

The group of 3- and 4-year-olds included children with developmental delays in relation to language, and team members were confident that the repeated story-reading throughout the week would support the children's development in this important area.

Gina took the book outside and soon a small group of children had gathered around her. Two children had even started to read the story themselves while she was catching up with Ashley's exciting news about his new baby.

Illustration 5.10: Bear Hunt 1 – the story

Gina praised the children for their reading and then read the story herself, attracting a growing group as the story progressed. Soon it was time to act out the story, beginning with the selection of a scarey bear. Nearly all the children wanted to take on this role, but Gina choose Elly. She had listened to the story attentively although she was sometimes an uninvolved listener at indoor storytimes. Elly ran off excitedly into the woodland area to find a cave to hide in.

Illustration 5.11: Bear Hunt 2 – the bear

Now it was time to search for the bear. Gina read each part of the story and modelled the actions: first wading through the long grass, then splashing through the deep river, next wading through the thick mud, and then stumbling through the dark forest.

Illustration 5.12: Bear Hunt 3 – the forest

It was all acted out with intense emotions and lots of vigorous movement. Some of the newer children stayed close to Gina, who wasn't quite sure if they were acting out being scared or were actually scared. Whichever it was, with the security that her presence provided, they were enjoying the experience.

Illustration 5.13: Bear Hunt 4 – 'We're not scared'

The part the children particularly enjoyed was the swirling snow-storm. Gina soon found she had as many as ten children who had all come together in the playground area to swirl and twirl until they were quite giddy. Finally the adventure came to an end and the bear ran away just before being caught. However, it wasn't actually the end as the children asked Gina to repeat the story-telling several times more during the outdoor play session.

As these case studies show, well-planned outdoor learning environments provide rich opportunities for learning but raise some specific planning issues. This chapter has presented a flexible approach to planning that includes positive strategies to support learning and teaching outdoors, while taking account of some key issues.

In the earlier discussion of curriculum frameworks, reference was made to the ways in which purposes and goals are shaped by diverse cultures and vary across curriculum frameworks (Spodek and Saracho 1996). The next chapter provides some contrasting and successful examples of approaches to planning an outdoor curriculum, shaped by very different cultural contexts.

Further Reading

Curtis, D. and Carter, M. (2003), *Design for Living and Learning.* St Paul, MN: Red Leaf Press.

Drake, J. (2001), *Planning Children's Play and Learning in the Foundation Stage.* London: David Fulton.

White, J. (2008), *Playing and Learning Outdoors.* Abingdon: Routledge.

6 | Outdoor learning in early-years curricula internationally

Each culture identifies the content of its education in relation to the knowledge it values, not just for personal growth, but because it reflects the society's view of what is true, what is right, what is beautiful. (Spodek and Saracho 1996, p. 11)

Outdoor play and learning is identified as an important strand of the early childhood curriculum in many countries. However, there are differences in approach and emphasis that reflect the contrasting values of different countries, shaped by 'cultural, economic, political and historic factors' (Ofsted 2003, p. 43). While it is not possible or appropriate to replicate in detail practice from very different cultural contexts, it is valuable to look at the ideas informing practice in other countries (Spodek and Saracho 1996; Ofsted 2003). Earlier in this book, an example of practice in a Japanese nursery was presented. This highlighted the cultural importance of natural world experiences for the very youngest children in Japan. This was a nursery where outdoor play for babies was a daily event. An example of innovative garden design for toddlers attending an American nursery has also been presented. Both these examples offer positive models of practitioners and a designer who place a high value on outdoor play for babies and toddlers. However, examples of babies and toddlers enjoying outdoor play in different cultural contexts are difficult to find, possibly reflecting a relatively widespread lack of attention to the affordances of outdoor play experiences for this age group. Therefore the examples below focus on the experiences of older children, from ages 3 to 6, and present three very different examples of successful outdoor learning from the contrasting cultural contexts of northern Italy, England and Norway.

The Villetta pre-school in Reggio Emilia

The first pre-school of Reggio Emilia, in northern Italy, was founded on Liberation Day in 1945, at the end of the war. The community of this town came together to build a pre-school from the rubble of destroyed buildings, creating a symbol of promise for a better future. Growing out of these special circumstances and following the defeat of fascism in Italy, the Reggio Emilia schools developed a unique philosophy. This distinctive approach, emphasizing the child as confident and competent, rich in potential, was developed by Loris Malaguzzi in collaboration with early-years educators, parents and the community (Penn 1997). It has inspired interest internationally.

One important strand within the Reggio Emilia philosophy is the emphasis on the physical environment and resources for children's learning (Dudek 2000). The environment, in interaction with children and resources, is seen as 'the third teacher'; it includes both the nursery garden and the wider environment of the town. Another important strand is the social-constructivist philosophy: children are encouraged to develop their thinking in the supportive social contexts provided by peers and teachers. One special outdoor project undertaken by 3–6-year-olds at Villetta pre-school, 'the amusement park for birds' (Reggio Children 1995), provides a fascinating example of these strands in practice.

Five- and six-year-olds initiated the idea for the project during a series of extensive class discussions around the needs of the birds that inhabited the school grounds. Having settled on the exciting idea of creating an amusement park for the birds, the children set out on their co-operative project. One of the children's important ideas was to provide fountains for the birds. The research therefore began with two field trips, where children observed, talked about, drew and photographed the beautiful fountains of their city. Following extensive discussion and drawing activity back in the pre-school, the children made models with clay, and painted and engaged in extended theorizing about the workings of the fountains. Finally, with the support of their teachers, the children were ready to experiment with water, pipes, tanks, sprays, water-wheels and a variety of other materials to create model fountains. Following an extended period of exploratory work, a variety of complex and beautiful fountains was constructed in the garden of the school, set out as an amusement park for the birds, and opened with a special community celebration.

It is the process of, first, developing ideas as a group, and second, communicating these through a range of languages that are two of the most important aspects of this outdoor project. As they work together through the different stages of the project, these children are developing a rich repertoire of 'logical, co-operative, expressive, imaginative and symbolic' languages (Reggio Children 1995, p. 16).

Images of the distinctive Reggio Emilia pre-schools and examples of the children's creative work can be found at the following URL: http://zerosei.comune.re.it/inter/nidiescuole.htm.

Forest Schools

From the very different culture of the Scandinavian countries, Forest Schools represent a further tradition with relevance for early childhood education. Currently, the ideals of the Forest School movement are having a growing impact on thinking about an outdoor curriculum for young children in the UK (Callaway 2005; Maynard 2007).

Forest Schools represent a significant strand of early childhood education in Norway, where physical education has a high status and where there is a strong and shared belief that young children should experience an active and outdoor childhood. The geography and climate of Norway help to explain the high value placed on educating children as confident and skilful citizens in outdoor environments. A high proportion of Norwegian early childhood settings offer children of up to 6 years of age extended periods of outdoor activities, active play and exercise. Many of these children gain experience of play, exercise and experiential learning within physically challenging environments and through all seasons of the year (OECD 1999).

Research in a Norwegian pre-school (Fjortoft 2001) has focused on the physical outcomes of Forest School experience, suggesting that challenging physical experiences can impact on the physical fitness of young children in positive ways. Fjortoft (2001) undertook quasi-experimental research with groups of 5- to 7-year-olds from three kindergartens. One kindergarten group enjoyed a wide variety of physical and creative play experiences and activities for one to two hours a day in a forest playscape situated at the edge of the kindergarten. The forest area included slopes, cliffs, rocks, plains and woodland vegetation. Children were allowed to play independently in the forest area closest to the kindergarten. In addition, adults accompanied them on regular visits further into the forest. In the other two kindergartens, children enjoyed similar periods of outdoor play, but in traditional outdoor play areas with standard playground equipment. Over the year of the study, children in the experimental group showed gradually improved motor ability in relation to the other groups, particularly in terms of children's balance and co-ordination. It seems that the natural landscape, compared with a traditional and well-equipped playground, increased opportunities for physical development.

Children who explored the more challenging forest playscape may have made further gains in their personal and emotional development, for example in self-confidence and a capacity to deal with risks. However, the Norwegian study (Fjortoft 2001) did not document learning of this kind. Concern for the social and emotional dimension of young children's experience has been particularly influential in the development of Forest Schools within the UK. Maynard (2007, p. 382) notes common British aims to first promote 'children's self-esteem, self-confidence and independence skills', and second, their sensitivity to and care for the environment. The Bridgwater Forest School in England and the Danish Forest Schools inspired Kernow Woodland Learning (Callaway 2005) in Cornwall, England, where nursery schoolchildren have half-day, weekly visits to a woodland 'classroom', playing outdoors in diverse weather conditions and through the changing seasons. While teachers plan games, activities and snack times that support children's development across six broad areas of learning, the project places a particular emphasis on the development of children's speaking and listening skills, alongside their social and emotional development. Formative records evidence significant behaviour shifts for individual children over the period of their visits to the woodland: 'Began quite withdrawn and not very enthusiastic ('Is it home time yet?'); later asked a lot more questions; loved the fire; able to take risks climbing trees' (Callaway 2005, p. 74).

Callaway (2005) explains how the distinctive practice of the Scandinavian Forest Schools has relevance for practitioners working in a very different cultural and environmental context. However, Maynard (2007), analysing data relating to a Forest School programme in South Wales, using a post-structuralism approach, notes some tensions between the philosophy of the Scandinavian Forest Schools, as represented by the perspectives of the Forest School workers, and the philosophy of the Welsh early-years teachers, working within a prescribed school curriculum. While the Forest School workers felt confident to promote the 'individuality, independence and freedom' (Maynard 2007, p. 388) of children in ways that might be taken for granted in a Scandinavian context, the Welsh teachers had other concerns. They were initially worried about the risks posed by some outdoor activities, seeing the children as in need of care and protection in a hazardous environment, and they felt uneasy about their lack of control over curriculum outcomes in the unfamiliar environment. Some tensions remained, although, over time, the two teachers gained a new understanding of the Forest School philosophy and began to see the potential gains for their children from this approach.

It seems that the distinctive practice of the Scandinavian Forest Schools has relevance for practitioners working in very different cultural contexts. To find out more about this approach, images and an account of the work of the Forest School movement in Suffolk, England, access http://www.bbc.co.uk/suffolk/content/articles/2006/03/23/nature_school_feature.shtml.

Growing Schools in England

The Growing Schools initiative represents another important strand of outdoor education. The tradition of growing vegetables and flowers with young children reaches back into the first half of the nineteenth century, with the educational work of Froebel (Herrington 2001). Funded by the British government, Growing Schools sets out to encourage schools for all age groups to make better use of outdoor environments for teaching and learning. Specific aims of the initiative include to increase children's awareness and understanding of farming and growing, to increase opportunities for first-hand experience, and to increase children's understanding of, and responsibility for, the environment (DfES 2002).

A Growing Schools Garden was set up at the Hampton Court Flower Show in 2002 to provide an inspiring model of a school garden, with contributions from 21 schools, including several early childhood settings. The contributions demonstrate how a small and barren playground can be transformed into a stimulating outdoor classroom, with imaginative and innovative ideas but with a minimum of expenditure. Young children and children with special educational needs were actively involved in the creation of the different elements of an inspiring garden. These included herbs and vegetables grown in decorated and recycled containers, bird-feeders and nest boxes, decorated pots and pans for a musical washing-line, and a multi-sensory interactive pergola. The Growing Schools initiative demonstrates how children's active participation in planning, designing and making a garden is essential if they are to develop a real sense of responsibility for the environment. It suggests that an educational garden should be designed as an evolving environment, with each new cohort of children contributing new ideas.

The Coombes Infants and Nursery School in Reading was one of the schools that participated in this garden project, and its environmental work, which is at the centre of the school curriculum, exemplifies this approach. Every child is involved throughout the year in the cycle of planting, growing and harvesting, for example, contributing to the school sunflower garden (Clark et al. 2003). Children are also involved in celebrating many festivals, and these often link to their work in the garden and wildlife areas. The outdoor environment is used in imaginative ways to engage children in significant experience. For example, at the Millennium, children, the staff and their families joined together for a night-time celebration outdoors that involved the lighting of 2,000 candles. The Coombes Infants and Nursery School demonstrates a meaningful link with the philosophy and practice of Froebel in the way in which it offers young children significant experiences in the outdoor environment, experiences that nurture a sense of both community and spirituality.

Images of active outdoor education at the Coombes Infants and Nursery School can be found at the following URL: http://www.thecoombes.com/frames.html.

Information about the Growing Schools initiative can be found at the following URL: http://www.growingschools.org.uk/.

Further Reading

Callaway, G. (2005), *The Early Years Curriculum: A View From Outdoors*. London: David Fulton.

DfES (2002), *Growing Schools*. London: DfES.

7 | Sources of advice, guidance and support

This book has presented many examples of practitioners who successfully nourish young children's learning in outdoor environments. High-quality practice can be found across a wide range of settings and in very different communities; it can be found in inner-city schools providing rich play environments in the smallest of yards, as well as in kindergartens set on the edge of the forest.

Creating outdoor environments for play and learning is challenging but rewarding. It takes time, and should be planned as a long-term project that evolves through a number of phases. A wide range of knowledge and skills underpins successful development work, and there are significant benefits in involving children, colleagues and families in the process. Additionally, a number of organizations, local and national, provide valuable advice, guidance and support. Some starting points are listed below.

Consulting with children

- Save the Children is an international organization that is concerned with children's rights and has particular expertise in consulting with children. Details of a number of relevant publications can be accessed at: http://www.savethechildren.org.uk/.

Developing the outdoor environment

- Learning through Landscapes is a UK charity that undertakes research, gives advice and encourages action to improve school and early-years settings' grounds as environments for learning. Details of its work and publications can be found at: www.ltl.org.uk/.
- Groundwork is a British environmental regeneration charity. It

supports environmental development work, particularly in the UK's most disadvantaged communities. Details about its work can be accessed at: http://www.groundwork.org.uk/.

- The British Trust for Conservation Volunteers is a British charity that works with people to bring about positive environmental change. It offers guidance and practical support to develop wildlife areas in the grounds of schools and other early-years settings. Information about the charity can be accessed at: http://www.btcv.org/.

- Evergreen is a Canadian charity and environmental organization that has a mandate to bring nature to the city through naturalization projects. Information about its work, including work in school grounds, can be accessed at: http://www.evergreen.ca/.

- The Natural Learning Initiative is an American organization, based at North Carolina State University. It aims to promote the importance of the natural environment in children's daily experience, through environmental design, action research, education and dissemination of information. Details of this work can be accessed at: http://www.naturalearning.org.

- The Edible Schoolyard is a non-profit programme, focused on a kitchen garden that is located on the campus of Martin Luther King Junior Middle School in Berkeley, California. The website provides a number of useful links. It can be accessed at: http://www.edibleschoolyard.org/about.html.

Developing inclusive outdoor environments

- Sensory Trust is a British charity that offers consultancy and advice on inclusive designs for outdoor environments. Information about the organization and its publications can be accessed at: http://www.sensorytrust.org.uk/.

- The Waisman Center University of Wisconsin-Madison provides a wide range of information about its Discovery Garden, an outdoor learning space for young children. The Discovery Garden has been developed as an inclusive play space and a model for early childhood professionals. Information about this garden and a wide range of inclusive outdoor play spaces can be accessed at: http://www.waisman.wisc.edu/dg/.

References

Adams, S., Alexander, E., Drummond, M. J. and Moyles, J. (2004), *Inside the Foundation Stage*. London: Association of Teachers and Lecturers.

Anning, A. (1997), *The First Years at School*. Buckingham: Open University.

Anning, A. and Edwards, A. (2006), *Promoting Children's Learning from Birth to Five*, 2nd edn. Maidenhead, Berkshire: Open University.

Athey, C. (2007), *Extending Thought in Young Children. A Parent–Teacher Partnership*, 2nd edn. London: Paul Chapman.

Aubrey, C., David, T., Godfrey, R. and Thomas, L. (2000), *Early Childhood Educational Research*. London and New York: RoutledgeFalmer.

Baldock, P. (2001), *Regulating Early Years Services*. London: David Fulton.

Bilton, H. (2002), *Outdoor Play in the Early Years: Management and Innovation*, 2nd edn. London: David Fulton.

Bishop, J. (2001), 'Creating places for living and learning', in L. Abbott and C. Nutbrown (eds), *Experiencing Reggio Emilia Implications for Pre-school Provision*. Buckingham and Philadelphia: Open University Press, pp. 72–9.

Bishop, K. (2001), 'Designing sensory play environments for children with special needs'. Paper presented to the IPA Conference 2001 (online). Last accessed on 13 August 2003 at http://pracv.asn.au/news.htm.

Boldermann, C., Blennow, M., Dal, H., Martensson, F., Raustorp, A., Yuen, K. and Wester, U. (2006), 'Impact of preschool environment on children's physical activity and sun exposure', in *Preventive Medicine*, 42, pp. 301–8.

Bradford Education (1995), *'Can I Play Out?' Outdoor Play in the Early Years*. Bradford: Bradford Education.

Bredecamp, S. (ed.) (1987), *Developmentally Appropriate Practice in Early Childhood Programs Serving Children from Birth Through Age 8*. Washington, DC: National Association for the Education of Young Children.

British Medical Journal (BMJ) (2001), 'Editorials. The obesity epidemic in young children', in *British Medical Journal*, 322, pp. 313–14. Last accessed on 29 December 2008 at www.bmj.com/cgi/content/full/322/7282/313.

Brooker, L. (2005), 'Learning to be a child. Cultural diversity and early years ideology', in N. Yelland (ed.), *Critical Issues in Early Childhood Education*. Maidenhead, Berkshire: Open University.

Bruce, T. (2005), *Early Childhood Education*, 3rd edn. London: Hodder Arnold.

Burdette, H. L. and Whitaker, R. C. (2005), 'Resurrecting free play in young children', in *Archives of Pediatric Adolescent Medicine*, 159, pp. 46–50.

Callaway, G. (2005), *The Early Years Curriculum: A View from Outdoors*. London: David Fulton.

Charlton, M. (2002), 'Sharing good practice: animal welfare. Hop to it!', *Nursery World*, 30 May 2002.

Clark, A. (2007), 'View from inside the shed: young children's perspectives of the outdoor environment', in *Education 3–13*, 35, (4), pp. 349–63.

Clark, A. (2008), *Why and How We Listen to Young Children*. London: National Children's Bureau.

Clark, A. and Moss, P. (2001), *Listening to Young Children: The Mosaic Approach*. London: National Children's Bureau.

Clark, A. and Moss, P. (2005), *Spaces to Play: More Listening to Young Children Using the Mosaic Approach*. London: National Children's Bureau.

Clark, A., McQuail, S. and Moss, P. (2003), *Exploring the Field of Listening to and Consulting with Young Children*. London: DfES.

Clark, A., Trine Kjørholt, A. and Moss, P. (2005), *Beyond Listening: Children's Perspectives on Early Childhood Services*. Bristol: Policy

Connolly, P. (1998), *Racism, Gender Identities and Young Children*. London and New York: Routledge.

Connolly, P. (2004), *Boys and Schooling in the Early Years*. London and New York: RoutledgeFalmer

Corsaro, W. (2005), *The Sociology of Childhood*, 2nd edn. Thousand Oaks, California: Pine Forge.

Curtis, D. and Carter, M. (2003), *Design for Living and Learning*. St Paul, MN: Red Leaf Press.

Dahlberg, G., Moss, P. and Pence, A. (eds) (2006), *Beyond Quality in Early Childhood Education and Care*, 2nd edn. London: Falmer.

Davis, J. M. and Elliot, S. (2004), 'Mud-pies and daisy chains: Connecting young children and nature', in *Every Child*, 10, (4), pp. 4–5.

DCSF (2008), *Practice Guidance for the Early Years Foundation Stage*. Nottingham: DCSF.

De Hann, D. and Singer, E. (2001), 'Young children's language of togetherness', in *International Journal of Early Years Education*, 9, (2), pp. 117–24.

DfEE (1990), *Starting With Quality: The Report of the Committee of Enquiry into the Quality of Educational Experience Offered to 3- and 4-year-olds*. London: HMSO.

DfES (2002), *Growing Schools*. London: DfES.

DfES (2004), *Every Child Matters: Change for Children*. London: DfES.

Diana Municipal Pre-school (1990), Diana Hop! Reggio Emilia: 'Diana' Municipal Pre-school.

Dickins, M. (2008), *Listening to Young Disabled Children*. London: National Children's Bureau.

Doctoroff, S. (2001), 'Adapting the physical environment to meet the needs of all young children for play', in *Early Childhood Education Journal*, 29, (2), pp. 105–9.

Drake, J. (2001), *Planning Children's Play and Learning in the Foundation Stage*. London: David Fulton.

Driscoll, V. and Rudge, C. (2005), 'Channels for listening to young children and parents', in A. Clark, A. T. Kjørholt and P. Moss (eds), *Beyond Listening*. Bristol: Policy Press.

Drummond, M. (2000), 'Comparisons in early years education' (online), *Early Childhood Research and Practice*, 2, (1). Last accessed on 10 February 2003 at http://ecrp.uiuc.edu/v2n1/drummond.html.

Dudek, M. (2000), *Kindergarten Architecture: Space for the Imagination*, 2nd edn. London: Spon Press.

Early Childhood Education Forum (1998), *Quality in Diversity in the Early Years*. London: National Children's Bureau.

Early Childhood Mathematics Group (2001), 'Foundation Stage Mathematics', in *Mathematics Teaching*, 175, pp. 20–2.

Edgington, M. (1998), *The Nursery Teacher in Action: Teaching 3, 4 and 5 year olds*. London: Paul Chapman.

Edgington, M. (2002), *The Great Outdoors*. London: Early Education.

Eisner, E. W. (1996), *Cognition and Curriculum Reconsidered*, 2nd edn. London: Paul Chapman.

Elfer, P., Goldschmied, E. and Selleck, D. (2003), *Key Persons in the Nursery*. London: David Fulton.

Elliot, L. (1999), *Early Intelligence: How the Brain and Mind Develop in the First Five Years of Life*. London: Penguin.

Ellis, N. (2002), *Firm Foundations? A Survey of ATL Members Working in the Foundation Stage*. London: Association of Teachers and Lecturers.

Fjortoft (2001), 'The natural environment as a playground for children: The impact of outdoor play activities in pre-primary school children', in *Early Childhood Education Journal*, 29, (2), pp. 11–117.

Franklin, B. (2002), *The New Handbook of Children's Rights*. London and New York: Routledge/Taylor and Francis Group.

Frost, J. L., Wortham, S. C. and Reifel, S. (2008), *Play and Child Development*, 3rd edn. Upper Saddle River, New Jersey: Pearson Education.

Gallahue, D. L. and Ozmun, J. C. (1998), *Understanding Motor Development: Infants, Children, Adolescents and Adults*, 4th edn. Boston, MA: McGraw-Hill.

Gelman, R. and Brenneman, K. (2004), 'Science learning pathways for young children', in *Early Childhood Research Quarterly*, 19, pp. 150–8.

Gill, T. (2008), 'Space-orientated children's policy: Creating child-friendly communities to improve children's well-being', in *Children and Society*, 22, pp. 136–42.

Graham, P. (2008), 'Susan Isaacs and the Malting House School', in *Journal of Child Psychotherapy*, 34, (1), pp. 5–22.

Great Ormond Street Hospital (2009), *Families First for Health: Sun Protection*. Last accessed 16 January 2009 at www.childrenfirst.nhs.uk/families/az_child_health/s/sun_protection.html.

Harms, T., Clifford, R. and Cryer, D. (1998), *Early Childhood Environment Rating Scale*, rev. edn. New York and London: Teachers College Press.

Hart, R. (1979), *Children's Experience of Place*. New York: Irvington Publishers.

Henry, J. (2003), 'Ministers launch new assault on gender gap', *Times Educational Supplement*, 17 January, 16.

Herrington, S. (2001), 'Kindergarten: Garden pedagogy from Romaticism to Reform', in *Landscape Journal*, 20, (1), pp. 30–4.

Herrington, S. (2005), 'The sustainable landscape', in M. Dudek (ed.), *Children's Spaces*. Oxford and Burlington MA 01803: Architectural Press.

Herrington, S. (2006), 'The design of landscapes at child-care centres: Seven Cs', in *Landscape Research*, 31, 1, pp. 63–82.

Herrington, S. (2008), 'Perspectives from the ground: Early childhood educators' perceptions of outdoor play spaces at child care centers', in *Children, Youth and Environments*, 18, (2), pp. 64–87.

Hestenes, L. and Carroll, D. (2000), 'The play interactions of young children with and without disabilities: Individual and environmental influences', *Early Childhood Research Quarterly*, 15, (2), pp. 229–46.

Hughes, S. (1992), *Sally's Secret*. London: Red Fox.

Isaacs, S. (1932), *The Nursery Years: The Mind of the Child from Birth to Six Years*. London: Routledge and Kegan Paul.

Keats, E. J. (1964), *Whistle for Willie*. London: Bodley Head.

Laevers, F. (2000), 'Forward to basics! Deep-level-learning and the experiential approach', in *Early Years*, 20, (2), pp. 20–9.

Lancaster, P. (2006), 'Listening to young children: Respecting the voice of the child', in G. Pugh and B. Duffy (eds), *Contemporary Issues in the Early Years*. London: Sage.

Learning through Landscapes (2003), *10 Years of Learning through Landscapes*. Winchester: LTL,

Liebschner, J. (2001), *A Child's Work Freedom and Guidance in Froebel's Educational Theory and Practice*. Cambridge: The Lutterworth Press.

Manning-Morton, M. and Thorp, M. (2003), *Key Times for Play*. Maidenhead, Berkshire: Open University.

Maynard, T. (2007), 'Encounters with Forest School and Foucault: A risky business?', in *Education 3–13*, 35, (4), pp. 379–91.

Maynard, T. and Waters, J. (2007), 'Learning in the outdoor environment: a missed opportunity?', in *Early Years*, 27, (3), pp. 255–65.

McNaughton, G. (2000), *Rethinking Gender in Early Childhood Education*. London: Paul Chapman.

McNaughton, G. and Hughes, P. (2009), *Doing Action Research in Early Childhood Studies*. Maidenhead, Berkshire: Open University.

McNaughton, G. and Williams, G. (2009), *Teaching Young Children: Choices in Theory and Practice*, 2nd edn. Maidenhead, Berkshire: Open University.

McNeish, D. and Scott, S. (2007), *The State of London's Children Report*. London: Greater London Authority.

Meade, A. (2006) 'New Zealand: the importance of outdoor space in education facilities for young children', in OECD (ed.), *Education Facilities for Young Children*, PEB Exchange, 2 June 2009 at: www.oecd.org/dataoecd/62/33/37697238.pdf.

Meade, A. and Cubey, P. (2008), *Thinking Children: Learning About Schemas*. Maidenhead, Berkshire: Open University.

Meade, A. and Ross, F. (2006), 'Education facilities for young children', *PEB Exchange, Programme on Educational Building, 2006/5*, OECD Publishing. DOI: 10.1787/407064601310.

Meadows, S. (1993), *The Child as Thinker*. London and New York: Routledge.

Miller, K. (1989), *The Outside Play and Learning Book*. Beltsville, Maryland: Gryphon House.

Millward, A. and Whey, R. (1997), *Facilitating Play on Housing Estates*. London: Chartered Institute of Housing and Joseph Rowntree Foundation.

Ministry of Education (1996), *Te Whāriki: He Whāriki Mātauranga mō ngā Mokopuna o Aotearoa: Early Childhood Curriculum*. Wellington: Learning Media.

Mooney, A., Boddy, J., Statham, J. and Warwick, I. (2008), 'Approaches to developing health in early years settings', in *Health Education*, 108, (2), pp. 163–77.

Morrow, V. (2002), 'Children's rights to public space', in B. Franklin (ed), *The New Handbook of Children's Rights*. London and New York: Routledge/ Taylor and Francis Group, pp. 168–81.

Moss, P. and Haydon, G. (2008), '*Every Child Matters* and the concept of education', in *Viewpoint*, 17, July 2008.

Nabhan, G. (1994a), 'A child's sense of wildness', in G. Nabhan and S. Trimble (1994), *The Geography of Childhood: Why Children Need Wild Places*. Boston, Massachusetts: Beacon Press, pp. 3–14.

Nabhan, G. (1994b), 'Children in touch, creatures in story', in G. Nabhan and S. Trimble (1994), *The Geography of Childhood: Why Children Need Wild Places*. Boston, Massachusetts: Beacon Press, pp. 77–107.

National Children's Bureau (2008), *Listening to and Consulting Young Children Project*. Last accessed 27 December 2008 at: www.ncb.org.uk/Page.asp? originx6668cx_211360867683c3p6773783809.

Nind, M. (2001), 'Enhancing the communication learning environment of an early years unit', *Education-Line* (online). Last accessed on 7 January 2003 at: www.leeds.ac.uk/educol/documents/00001920.htm.

Norton, C., Nixon, J. and Sibert, J. R. (2004), 'Playground injuries to children', in *Archives of Disease in Childhood*, 39, pp. 103–8.

OECD (1999), *OECD Country Note Early Childhood Education and Care Policy in Norway* (online). Last accessed on 25 February at: www.oecd.org/pdf/ M00020000/M0020292.pdf.

OECD (2006), *Starting Strong 2 Early Childhood Education and Care*. Paris: OECD.

Ofsted (2001), *Nursery Education: Quality of Provision for 3- and 4-year-olds 2000–2001*. London: Ofsted.

Ofsted (2003), *The Education of Six-year-olds in England, Denmark and Finland*. London: Ofsted.

Ofsted (2008), *Early Years Leading to Excellence* (online). Last accessed 27 December 2008 at: www.ofsted.gov.uk/Ofsted-home/Leading-to-excellence.

Ojala, M. (2005), 'How Finland is researching early childhood education', in B. Spodek and O. N. Saracho (eds), *International Perspectives on Research in Early Childhood Education*. Greenwich, Connecticut: Information Age Publishing.

Ouvry, M. (2000), *Exercising Muscles and Minds: Outdoor Play and the Early Years Curriculum*. London: The National Early Years Network.

Parke, R. D. (2004), 'The Society for Research in Child Development at 70: Progress and promise', in *Child Development*, 75, (1), pp. 1–24.

Pascal, C. and Bertram, T. (1997), *Effective Early Learning: Case Studies in Improvement*. London: Hodder and Stoughton.

Pascal, C., Bertram, T., Gaspar, M., Mould, C., Ramsden, F. and Saunders, M. (2001), *Research to Inform the Evaluation of the Early Excellence Centres Pilot Programme*. London: DfEE.

Penn, H. (1997), 'Where do good ideas come from?', in P. Gura (ed.), *Reflections on Early Education and Care*. London: Early Education.

Perry, J. (2001), *Outdoor Play: Teaching Strategies with Young Children*. New York: Teachers College Press.

Raban, B., Ure, C. and Waniganayake, M. (2003), 'Multiple perspectives: acknowledging the virtue of complexity in measuring quality', in *Early Years*, 23, (1), pp. 67–77.

Rayna, S. (2004), 'Professional practices with under-ones in French and Japanese day care centres', in *Early Years*, 24, (1), pp. 35–47.

Reggio Children (1995), *Le Fontane: The Fountains*. Reggio Emilia, Italy: Reggio Children S. r. l.

Rich, D. (2008), *Listening to Babies*. London: National Children's Bureau.

Rishbeth, C. (2004), 'Ethno-cultural representation in the urban landscape', in *Journal of Urban Design*, 9, (3), pp. 311–33.

Robb, M. (2001), 'The changing experience of childhood', in P. Foley, J. Roche and S. Tucker (eds), *Children in Society*. Basingstoke, Hampshire: Palgrave.

Roche, J. (2002), 'The Children Act 1989 and children's rights: a critical reassessment', in B. Franklin (ed.), *The New Handbook of Children's Rights*. London and New York: Routledge/Taylor and Francis Group.

Rosen, M. and Oxenbury, H. (1993), *We're Going on a Bear Hunt*. London: Walker Books.

Rushton, S. and Larkin, E. (2001), 'Shaping the learning environment: Connecting developmentally appropriate practices to brain research', in *Early Childhood Education Journal*, 29, (1), pp. 25–33.

Salmon, P., Taggart, B., Smees, R., Sylva, K., Melhuish, E., Siraj-Blatchford, I. and Eliot, K. (2003), *The Early Years Transition and Special Educational Needs (EYTSEN) Project*. London: DfES.

Sammons, P., Taggart, B., Smees, R., Sylva, K., Melhuish, E., Siraj-Blatchford, I. and Eliot, K. (2003), *The Early Years Transition and Special Educational Needs (EYTSEN) Project*. Research Report RR431. Nottingham: DCSF.

Schaffer, H. R. (1996), *Social Development*. Oxford: Blackwell.

Senda, M. (1992), *Design of Children's Play Environments*. New York: McGraw-Hill.

Sharp, C. (2003), 'School starting age: European policy and recent research', in *Early Education*, Spring 2003.

Shell, E. R. (2003), *The Hungry Gene: The Science of Fat and the Future of Thin*. New Delhi: Atlantic Books.

Singer, E. (2002), 'The logic of young children's (nonverbal) behaviour', in *European Early Childhood Education Research Journal*, 10, (1), pp. 55–65.

Siraj-Blatchford, J. and Siraj-Blatchford, I. (2003), *Supporting Information and*

Communication Technology in the Early Years. Buckingham: Open University Press.

Siraj-Blatchford, I. and Sylva, K. (2004), 'Researching pedagogy in English pre-schools', in *British Educational Research Journal*, 30, 5, pp. 713–30.

Siraj-Blatchford, I., Sylva, K., Muttock, S., Gilden, R. and Bell, D. (2002), *Researching Effective Pedagogy in the Early Years*. London: DfES.

Smith, P. K., Cowie, H. and Blades. M. (2003), *Understanding Children's Development*, 4th edn. Oxford: Blackwell.

Spodek, B. and Saracho, O. (1996), 'Culture and the early childhood curriculum', in *Early Child Development and Care*, 123, pp. 1–13.

Steedman, C. (1990), *Childhood, Culture and Class in Britain: Margaret McMillan, 1860–1931*. London: Virago.

Stephenson, A. (2002), 'Opening up the outdoors: Exploring the relationship between the indoor and outdoor environments of a centre', in *European Early Childhood Education Research Journal*, 10, (1), pp. 29–38.

Stephenson, A. (2003), 'Physical risk-taking: Dangerous or endangered?', in *Early Years*, 23, (1), pp. 35–43.

Stoneham, J. (1996), *Grounds for Sharing* (online). Godalming, Surrey: Learning Through Landscapes. Book from Education Resources Information Centre. Last accessed 17 January 2009 at: http://eric.ed.gov/ERICDocs/data/ericdocs2sql/content_storage_01/0000019b/80/16/22/b7.pdf.

Stoneham, J. (1997), 'Health benefits', in *Landscape Design*, February 1997, pp. 23–6.

Sutton-Smith, B. (1997), *The Ambiguity of Play*. Cambridge, MA and London: Harvard University Press.

Sylva, K., Roy, C. and Painter, M. (1980), *Childwatching at Playgroup and Nursery School*. London: Grant McIntyre.

Talbot, J. and Frost, J. L. (1989), 'Magical landscapes', in *Childhood Education*, 66, pp. 11–15.

Thomas, N. (2001), 'Listening to children', in P. Foley, J. Roche and S. Tucker (eds), *Children in Society*. Basingstoke, Hampshire: Palgrave.

Thomson, S. (2005), '"Territorialising" the primary school playground: Deconstructing the geography of playtime', in *Children's Geographies*, 3, (1), pp. 63–78.

Titman, W. (1994), *Special Places; Special People: The Hidden Curriculum of School Grounds*. Godalming, Surrey: WWF UK/Learning Through Landscapes.

Trimble, S. (1994), 'The scripture of maps, the names of trees: A child's landscape', in G. Nabhan and S. Trimble (eds), *The Geography of Childhood. Why Children Need Wild Places*. Boston, Massachusetts: Beacon Press, pp. 15–31.

Waite, S. (2007), '"Memories are made of this": some reflections on outdoor learning and recall', in *Education 3–13*, 35, (4), pp. 333–47.

Wake, S. J. (2007), 'Designed for learning: Applying "learning-informed design" for children's gardens', in *Applied Environmental Education and Communication*, 6, pp. 31–8.

Walsh, D. (2005), 'Developmental theory and early childhood education', in N. Yelland (ed.), *Critical Issues in Early Childhood Education*. Maidenhead, Berkshire: Open University.

Wells, G. (1987), *The Meaning Makers: Children Learning Language and Using Language to Learn*. London: Hodder and Stoughton.

Welsh Assembly Government (2008), *Play/Active Learning. Overview for 3- to 7-year-olds*. Cardiff: The National Assembly for Wales.

Welsh Assembly Government (2008), *The Foundation Phase Framework for 3- to 7-year-olds in Wales*. Cardiff: The National Assembly for Wales.

White, J. (2008), *Playing and Learning Outdoors*. Abingdon, Oxon: Routledge.

Williams, G. M. (1994), 'Talk on the climbing frame', in *Early Child Development and Care*, 102, pp. 81–9.

Wood, D., McMahon, L. and Cranstoun, Y. (1980), *Working With Under-fives*. London: Grant McIntyre.

Wood, E. (2007), 'New directions in play: consensus or collision', in *Education 3–13*, 35, 4, pp. 309–20.

Wood, E. and Attfield, J. (2005), *Play, Learning and the Early Childhood Curriculum*, 2nd edn. London: Paul Chapman.

Wood, P. and Yearley, D. (2007), *Growing Spaces for Play: The Value of Playing in the Natural Environment*, 2nd edn. Faringdon: Playsafety Ltd.

Woodward, R. J. and Yun, J. (2001), 'The performance of fundamental gross motor skills by children enrolled in Head Start', in *Early Child Development and Care*, 169, pp. 57–67.

Woolley, H. (2008), 'Watch this space: Designing for children's play in public open spaces', in *Geography Compass*, 2, (20), pp. 495–512.

Index

Action research 9. 43, 122
Adult role 23, 25, 27, 39, 59, 106
Animals 3, 7, 17, 100–2
Australia 59

Biological concepts 17–18
Book corner 90
Books 100, 103–4, 108–9
British Trust for Conservation Volunteers 122

Canadian x, 50, 122
Children's voices 1
City 7, 25, 36, 50, 100, 103, 116, 121, 122
Climbing 3, 9, 16, 25, 56, 69, 71, 89, 118
Collections 33–4
Conflict 43–6, 60, 81, 104
Construction 9, 26, 51, 53, 56, 88, 89, 92–7
Creative 10, 14, 55, 62, 78, 89, 98, 117
Critical theory 31–2
Cross-cultural studies 57–8

Denmark x
Dens 51–2, 98, 100–1
Disabled children 61–4, 71

Elementary school tradition 13–14, 16, 24
Emotional well-being 8, 17, 18, 33, 41–3, 76–7, 78, 115, 118–19
England x, xi, 1, 8, 10, 16, 31, 33, 37, 54, 76, 78–81, 93, 115
Environmental change 8, 122
Environmental understanding 7
Environmental responsibility 7, 34, 76
Europe 14–15, 17

Evaluation 34, 63, 77, 96, 105
Every Child Matters 8, 33, 37, 78
Experiential education ix, 76–7, 79, 100
Exploratory play 83

Families viii, 17, 25, 28, 31–2, 67, 77, 120, 121
Finland 75
Forest schools 117–19
France x
French 29, 31, 43–4
Froebel ix, 15, 16–19, 119–20

Garden ix, xi, 2, 3, 13–19, 22, 27, 30, 32, 34–5, 42, 47, 49–50, 53, 55–6, 61–2, 67, 76, 80–1, 83–6, 90, 98–101, 106, 115–16, 119–20, 122
Gender 10–11, 36–9, 56–60, 71
Geographical perspectives 5, 33
Growing Schools 119–20

Health x–xi, 7–9, 15, 17–18, 24, 30, 33, 50–1, 68, 77, 79, 101
Health and safety 24, 68

ICT 98–9
Inclusive 39, 122
Inclusion 60–4
India 11
Infants 11, 28, 83
Isaacs, Susan 17–19
Italy 115–16

Japan 11, 15, 29–31, 44, 69, 115

Kenya 11
Kindergarten 15, 19, 64, 67, 81, 85, 117–18, 121

131

Language 9, 11, 16, 22, 26, 30, 60, 66, 67, 78, 80–1, 97
Learning dispositions 11, 93
Learning through Landscapes 121
Listening to children 64–7

McMillan, Margaret ix, 16–17, 19
Mental health 15
Memories 2–4
Messy play 39, 54–6
Mexico 11
Monitoring 96–8
Montessori, Maria ix
Mosaic approach 6
Music 89

Natural landscape 83
Natural materials 9, 88
Natural world 6–7, 48, 115
Netherlands 76
New Zealand 11, 34, 76–8
Norway x, 115, 117–18
Number 90
Nursery school 16

Observation 92, 97, 104
Organisation for Economic Co-operation and Development (OECD) x

Parents 3, 16, 29, 31
Pathways 84–5
Peer cultures 35–7, 55
Percussion instruments 10
Personal spaces 6
Philippines 11
Physical challenge 39, 68–71
Physically active play 8, 11
Physical play area 89
Physical fitness 117
Piaget 24–8
Planning 71–113
Plants 85
Playgrounds 14
Playtimes 13
Playwork perspectives 37–8
Profile 103–4
Programme structure 39–43
Psychological development 16
Psychological perspectives 22–33, 57–8

Racism 36
Reggio Emilia ix, 81, 116–17
Rights 1, 65
Roadway 90
Role play 89

Save the Children 121
Scale 10, 55, 90–1
Scaffolding 29–30, 48
Schema 25–6, 38
Scientific concepts 27, 48
Scotland 16
Sensory experiences 5, 6, 10, 16, 62
Sensory Trust 122
Shelter 16
Small apparatus 89
Social experiences 5
Sociological perspectives 35–7
Social spaces 6
Social play 36
Special educational needs 60–3
Spiritual 15–18
Sustained shared thinking 30, 73
Sweden x

The Edible Schoolyard 122
The Natural Learning Initiative 122
The Waisman Centree 122
Therapeutic 15
Transporting schema 9

United States ix, 7, 8, 11, 14, 16, 27, 34, 81, 85

Vegetable garden 17

Wales ix, xi, 74, 81
Water play 86–7
Weather 39, 46–54, 106
Well-being 7
Wildflower gardens 16
Wild area 85–6
Wild places 33
Wildlife 62, 85

Zoning 84